the Manipulator and the Church

the Manipulator and the Church

MAXIE D. DUNNAM
GARY J. HERBERTSON
EVERETT L. SHOSTROM

ABINGDON PRESS ⓒ Nashville and New York

THE MANIPULATOR AND THE CHURCH

Copyright © 1968 by Abingdon Press

Library of Congress Catalog Card Number: 68-27627

SET UP, PRINTED, AND BOUND BY THE
PARTHENON PRESS, AT NASHVILLE,
TENNESSEE, UNITED STATES OF AMERICA

To Our Wives
Jerry, Nancy, and Donna

Acknowledgments

We would like to thank the following people who have assisted in different ways in the preparation of this manuscript:

Mrs. Susan Bell, Dr. Dale Baillie, and the Rev. Ralph Reynolds, who read the manuscript and provided helpful criticism;

members of the Christian Actualization Groups with whom many of the concepts here were "tested" and through whom much of the suggested "dynamics" was evolved;

those who have shared their personal "testimonies," some of which are included in the text;

Alvina Otwell, who deciphered our scribbling and typed the manuscript;

our wives and children, who provided ease and freedom for us to pursue this task—often on *their* time;

our congregations, counselees, and staffs, who continue to inspire and assist us in our personal growth.

For all of these we are grateful and here acknowledge the humanness they provided without which the book would not have been possible.

Maxie D. Dunnam
Gary J. Herbertson
Everett L. Shostrom

Contents

Introduction

The waters of the Christian church are troubled. The very foundations of the variegated institutions which claim allegiance to Christ are being shaken. On one hand there is talk about *New Life in the Church*. On the other hand there is much discussion about *The Death of God*. Some feel that we may be in the midst of *A New Reformation*, and others are convinced that we are moving toward *A World Come of Age*, a *Secular City* without religion. Some feel that the problem is the *Enemy in the Pew* while others say it is *The Empty Pulpit*.

In the midst of the turmoil of our time we feel that a clear word to the church as an institution and to Christians as individuals is needed. We are seeking to speak such a word.

It is our firm conviction that psychology and religion can and should work hand in hand to guide man in his quest for greater fulfillment. The psychologist believes in the dignity and worth of the human being. What is the source of this dignity and worth if it is not in man's spiritual nature? We have followed some of the concepts of Abraham Maslow, and in a real sense this volume is a sequel to *Man, the Manipulator*, by Everett L. Shostrom.

Manipulation is that which destroys a man as a man. *Actu-*

alization in its fullness is the experience of the kingdom which God means for all of us to enter.

The theories of actualization and manipulation touch every aspect of the life of the church: theology, polity, worship, prayer, administration, personal relationships. The church needs to have stripped from it all systems of manipulation to make room for actualization. The sad fact is that the church is alive with manipulation and may soon be dead because of it.

The traditional church has often made man the *means* for the *end*—the church. Christian actualization requires that the church and its program become the *means* for man and his actualization.

Actualization is a *life* program which embraces the institution of the church but is not limited to the program of the church. Until we can subordinate our institutional needs to making the fulfillment of man our ultimate goal, we will never realize Jesus' ideal for human life and his church.

Our effort here is in part a confession of our own manipulations. It is also a testament of faith. We will seek to do two things: One, to indicate the areas of our failures and manipulations, and two, to propose a concept of a "Christian actualizing style of life" and "an actualization-centered church."

Hopefully, the reader will hear and respond to "the call to Christian actualization."

We believe that this book can be of value to all clergy and laity. It may be strong medicine for some, but for all we hope it will inspire a new look at some old and worn practices. For the nonchurch member and the church critic we also hope it will be of interest, for this book shows that the church can subject itself to honest self-examination and in so doing, create dialogue and speak a convincing word. The church should be glad for its enemies and critics—it can *learn* from them. For nonmembers and critics here is a fresh word that can stir their interest and speak relevantly to them. We also hope that this book will provide direction for all who wish to see their church become more vital and actualizing.

Maxie D. Dunnam
Gary J. Herbertson
Everett L. Shostrom

Chapter I
The Human Predicament

Manipulation

Man is a manipulator. He is the creator and the perpetuator of a vast manipulative system. Manipulation has become the *modus operandi* of our modern civilization. The con man has become the prototype of success. The system and the man are glorified because they "produce results," they "deliver the goods."

The manipulator is legion. He is all of us, consciously, subconsciously, or unconsciously employing all the phony tricks we absorb between the cradle and the crematory to conceal the actual vital nature of ourselves—and, in the process, reducing ourselves and our fellow man into things to be controlled. A recent movie entitled *The Incredible Shrinking Man* is a parable of our plight. It is the story of a man who shrinks to such a tiny size that he has to fight a spider with a pin. This is the same kind of loss of perspective that has come from man's manipulation.

On his first day at college a young man was filling out the barrage of registration forms in a large room surrounded by

15

several hundred other students. Across the table from him were two professors, advisors for entering students. "I wonder how many new bodies we have this year?" one asked the other. The professor may have been facetious, but the young man's feelings of insecurity were heightened. He went away feeling the brunt of our impersonal system. He was a thing—a body—someone to fill up a seat in the freshman class of Introduction to Psychology.

This is the result of the complex manipulative patterns that characterize our relationships. Man is dehumanized. This is what a manipulator is: "One who exploits, uses, and/or controls himself and others as things or objects." Viktor E. Frankl has dramatically illustrated the struggle of man against the maneuvering, using, controlling forces that would reduce him to less than a man. As a longtime prisoner of the brutal concentration camps of Nazi Germany he found himself stripped to naked existence and face to face daily with that which would rob him of the very essence of himself. "How could he—every possession lost, every value destroyed, suffering from hunger, cold and brutality, hourly expecting extermination—how could he find life worth preserving?"

In his book *Man's Search for Meaning* he tells of his first day in prison, which set the stage for the terrifying struggle that he was to know and the endless days that were to follow. The prisoners were told to leave their luggage on the train and to fall into two lines—women on one side, men on the other. They were to file past a senior S. S. officer in whose hands their destiny lay. Frankl describes the casual attitude of this officer to his task: "He had assumed an attitude of careless ease, supporting his right elbow with his left hand. His right hand was lifted, and with the forefinger of that hand he pointed very leisurely to the right or to the left. None of us had the slightest idea of the sinister meaning behind that little movement of a man's finger. . . . The significance of the finger game was explained to us in the evening. It was the first selection, the first verdict, made on our existence or non-existence." [1]

Later on that evening Frankl inquired of a prisoner who had been there for some time where a certain colleague and friend had been sent. He was asked, "Was he sent to the left side?" When Frankl responded "yes," the prisoner said, "Then you can see him there," and he pointed to a chimney a few hundred yards away which was sending a sinister cloud of smoke into the gray sky of Poland. "That's where your friend is, floating up to Heaven."

The terrible movement of the S. S. officer's finger dawned upon Frankl. Ninety percent of his transport group had been sent to the crematorium. Frankl was to learn during the awful days that followed that the movement of a finger was a symbol of a man being completely controlled, used, and reduced to a subhuman thing. Though perhaps not to this extreme, this movement of the finger is a symbol of the manipulation in which every man is caught.

The finger of Madison Avenue points in a certain direction and 200 million Americans are expected to follow. An automobile is sold through the manipulation of a fantasy and wish fulfillment. A sexy blonde is pictured at the wheel as though this were a part of owning the car. A cigarette is sold as a passport to masculinity. The finger of the "in" set points in the direction of youthful virility, and senior citizens begin

[1] (New York: Washington Square Press, 1963) pp. 17-18.

to do the watusi and race to the fountain of youth expressed through cosmetics and gay teen-age apparel.

The finger of middle-class America points to the church as a place to belong if one would be socially acceptable. Good citizenship and good religion are made synonymous. The "pew" becomes "comfortable," and prophetic proclamation is replaced by the "noise of solemn assemblies." A good portion of the population is identified with some religious group, but one may legitimately wonder about the meaning of this identity.

These are only a few of the fingers of manipulation which exploit, use, and/or control people as things or objects. The result is seen in the frustration and despair which characterize our existence. Man has come to view himself as a consumer. He becomes less and less a thinking and deciding and feeling man. He becomes more a passive man—doing what he is told to do, buying what he is told to buy, and feeling what he is told to feel. His personhood shrinks. To the extent that he responds to the direction of the finger of manipulation he builds a false self. Because he has been unpatriotic to his real self, he belongs nowhere and to no one.

Many alternatives are available to modern man and to the modern church. In this book we are contending that there are two basic alternatives that press for a decision. The alternatives are *manipulation* or *actualization*. These are really styles of life, or stances toward life. To our self-defeat we have often adopted the manipulative style.

To see these styles of life in contrast will assist us in perspective. The four fundamental characteristics of the manipulator are deception, unawareness, control, and cynicism. Look at these in turn.

The Primary Characteristics of Manipulation

DECEPTION

The manipulator is basically deceptive. He uses tricks, techniques, and maneuvers because he cannot trust the other person's honesty of motivation. So he puts on an act, plays roles in order to create an impression. His expressed feelings are deliberately chosen to fit the occasion. This means that he is never expressive of his true self, nor does he give another the opportunity to express his true self.

Test it in your own experience. How seldom are the occasions when you are really free in your relationship with another! How often have you felt, when in conversation with another, that every word was guarded, every sentence properly put, and every emotion completely controlled? How few have been the times, even in a whole life, that you have been able to say, "Gee, wasn't that great! I was completely free. I really let my hair down—I was my real self!"

A minister and his wife recalled two recent experiences that illustrate this. They had the occasion to visit in the homes of two minister friends on successive evenings. After the second evening as they drove away from the home, they blurted out, almost simultaneously "Wasn't that great! How different from last night!" And then they spent the forty-five minutes it took to drive home talking of the difference in the evenings. Unconsciously perhaps, victims of habit, caught in the clutches of manipulation, neither couple was free on the first evening. They guarded against self-exposure—deliberately chose feelings to fit the occasion.

Instance could be piled upon instance of deception charac-

19

terizing our lives and relationships as we have given ourselves to manipulation.

UNAWARENESS

Not only is the manipulator deceptive, he is unaware of the really important concerns of living. He has so focused on competing and winning that he misses everything but the game. He has what may be called "tunnel vision." There are no wide-angle lenses in his photographic sense equipment. He handles all of life with gloves, afraid of the real touch.

Frances Cornford, granddaughter of Charles Darwin, wrote a poem about it.

> O why do you walk through the fields in gloves,
>   Missing so much and so much?
> O fat white woman whom nobody loves,
> Why do you walk through the fields in gloves,
> When the grass is soft as the breast of doves
>   And shivering-sweet to the touch?
> O why do you walk through the fields in gloves,
>   Missing so much and so much? [2]

The poem was entitled "To a Fat Lady Seen from the Train" and, as Halford Luccock has reminded us, there may have been a dozen good reasons for the gloves. The poet may have been unfair to the lady, but the point is clear. Going through life with gloves we miss so much—in fact, we miss everything!

That's what happens to the manipulator. Unawareness is one of his primary characteristics, and so life, quivering in its

[2] Used by permission of Cresset Press Ltd., London.

reality and pulsating with warmness, passes him by. He passes it by! Playing only the game of the moment, he misses the big game of life.

CONTROL

A third characteristic of manipulation is control. For the manipulator, the understanding of human nature is for this one purpose: that he may control it. He conceals his motives, his feelings, and his attitudes. He plays life like a game of chess, deliberately feeling and responding in a fashion to fit the occasion. There is no spontaneity, no free flowing of feeling and response.

This effort at control is spreading like a prairie fire throughout culture. Bill is a supervisor in a division of state government that involves a number of civil servants. He has been sensitive to this problem of control, made aware of it in "sensitivity training." The state prescribed a course for all supervisory personnel, and Bill's comment was that it was a "brainwashing program of manipulation." New and sophisticated techniques of control were presented in order that the supervisors might be more *productive* with those over whom they were responsible. It has even happened in psychology, the discipline that is supposed to free a man. A psychologist of some note was reported to have said, "The truth is, we are trying to tell people what to do and make them think it was their idea." Not to help a man to be more himself but to control him!

Few are free. Wives and husbands, parents and children, salesmen and customers, ministers and parishioners—all are seeking control. We often evade real, honest, open *contact*. This is too spontaneous, too unpredictable. And so we miss the vital thing about people and about ourselves. Our real selves never meet with each other.

CYNICISM

The fourth characteristic of manipulation is cynicism. The manipulator is basically distrusting of himself and others. Deep down he doesn't trust human nature. More damaging, he can't trust his own ability to cope with others and situations. Thus his cynicism is not only directed to others, but to himself as well.

We often think we are free of this because we *talk* such a good game. We use a barrage of words in reference to our trust and understanding of human nature. We talk about the importance of love in human relationships, but do we really love? Reuel Howe has reminded us that we use our knowledge about love as an evasion of our responsibility to really love. "We can be so frightened by the risks of expressing love that we may turn away from those who need our love and have a right to expect it from us. How much easier and safer it is to know *about* God and his love and to confine this meaning to the sanctuary and the study group!" [3]

In our manipulative cynicism we *play it safe*. We take no risks in relationships where trust is involved. How often have you been warned, "Don't get involved with that person"? Or, how often have you warned others in the same way? One of two things has happened here. Either the person being warned against has taken another *in* and manipulated him, or the person giving the warning is fearsome of a trusting relationship and has settled into the cynicism of "playing it safe."

[3] *Herein Is Love* (Valley Forge, Pa.: Judson Press, 1961), p. 23.

It was Reuel Howe again who suggested that *moralism* in religion is really a technique of "playing it safe." The music of Jesus' message was offbeat to the religious men of his day for this very reason. He was saying to them that they were missing the life-giving freedom of proper relationships with God and with one another because they had reduced religion to *moralism*. This is the reason they decided to get rid of him.

When we reduce life to the dimensions of a moral code, as the religious men of Jesus' day had done and as many of us so happily do, we immediately freeze the Spirit. Actually, we do it because we are afraid to trust the Spirit and risk the dangers of love and trust and communication. When we turn life into a code and freeze that code into "proper religious living," we can be free of any responsibility to run any risks and enter into any uncertain relationships. We live by the "book," no questions asked—and so we play it safe! Moralistic religion becomes the soil out of which the seeds of manipulative cynicism grow. And the fruit of this seed is distrust and, eventually, despair.

Deception, unawareness, control, and *cynicism*—these are the characteristics of manipulation which, when incorporated in our lives and in our relationships, set fires of hell ablaze. When we adopt these characteristics as our styles of life, we have succumbed to the finger of manipulation and are on our swift way to self-defeat. The alternative is actualization.

Actualization

An actualizing person is an individual who appreciates himself and others as persons of unique worth and potential. At his height he is the opposite of the full manipulator. In varying degrees all of us are manipulators, and all of us are actualizors. It is one of the contentions of this book that out of the raw clay of the manipulator may be molded the actualizor, and a congregation bound in the fetters of manipulation may break forth into the freedom of actualization.

Jesus understood the many-splendored aspect of persons as no religious leader before ever had. Any religion true to his spirit must make this foundational assumption. He recognized in human nature a truth which Luther Burbank discovered in the plant realm; every weed is a potential flower. The very qualities which make it a weed can also make it a flower. When you look at the men whom Jesus chose as disciples, you will find this verified. They were for the most part men of amazing vigor. They had what Wallace Hamilton has called "earthy vitamins." Some of them were stormy men with turbulent passions, ambitious, with fighting instincts. Others were retiring men who shunned the limelight. All of them were different, and Jesus came not to destroy the powers and the passions of men, but to bring them to fulfillment.

Christian actualization is just that! It is a commitment to a style of life that purposely seeks to actualize one's true self, rather than to succumb to the phony roles of the manipulator. In chapter IV we will show how the actualizing person is a combination of potentials.

An actualizor is one who expresses his *actual* self and accepts the expression of other *actual* selves. Meister Eckhart, the great Christian mystic, expressed it this way:

> That I am a man,
> this I share with other men.
> That I see and hear and
> that I eat and drink

is what all animals do likewise.
But that I am I is only mine
and belongs only to me
and to nobody else;
to no other man
not to an angel nor to God—
except inasmuch
as I am one with Him.[4]

Martin Buber, to whom we are greatly indebted and on whose work *Man, the Manipulator* [5] is partially based, has described the contrast between a manipulative and an actualizing relationship as the difference between an "I-it" and an "I-thou" relationship. In our understanding a manipulative relationship is an "it-it" relationship, and an actualizing relationship is a "thou-thou" relationship. A person who regards another as an "it" becomes an "it"; and he who regards another as a "thou" becomes a "thou."

Many live according to the myth that whenever we are controlling others we are doing ourselves good. The truth is that to manipulate another is to reduce oneself to a "thing" and limit one's potential for meaningful *human* contact. The manipulator devalues and thus defeats himself as a person by his manipulative action.

The same is true in actualization. Treating another as a "thou" calls forth the depth of our being, the unique characteristics of our selfhood.

[4] "That I Am a Man," *Fragments*. Quoted in Erich Fromm, *Man for Himself* (New York: Holt, Rinehart and Winston, 1947), p. 38.
[5] Everett L. Shostrom (Nashville: Abingdon Press, 1967).

The Primary Characteristics of Actualization

HONESTY

The actualizing person is able to express himself and his feelings honestly—in fact to *be* his feelings in a genuine fashion. Having found meaning, direction, and purpose in his own existence, the actualizing person is not under the depressing burden of seeking to be something that he isn't. Growing in our actualizing style of life, we are constantly faced with the challenge of transparency or authenticity. Every day we are confronted with whether we will conceal our authentic being behind the various masks that are available to us, or permit our fellow men to see and know us as we are.

Almost every day the minister or professional counselor is brought face to face with the failure of people to be honest. People will say, "You are the first person I have ever been completely honest with." Or, "I have never told this to another person before today." There is ample reason to believe that this failure to be honest is one of the real causes of emotional problems. Constantly pretending to be something that we aren't carries with it a price too steep to pay. The actualizing person realizes this and accepts the fact that deception and concealment or, deeper than that, deliberate "phoniness" is not the natural state of man. Rather, self-disclosure is the more natural stance and contributes most to personal well-being, mental and spiritual health.

There is adequate reason for us to suspect from our counseling that a person begins to lose meaning, and life becomes a drudgery and an ordeal to the degree that he, by deception, conceals himself and his true identity from his fellows. A

26

person who is estranged from others and distrusts them to the point of misleading them into thinking that they know him when, in fact, they do not loses immeasurably in depth, and life becomes more and more a masquerade. In his study *The Transparent Self*, Sidney M. Jourard reminds us that "man, perhaps alone of all living forms, is capable of *being* one thing and *seeming* from his actions and talk to be something else. Not even those animals and insects and fishes which Nature expertly camouflages can do this 'seeming' at will; they do it reflexly." [6] The actualizing person has become sensitive to the subtle attractiveness of this trap—to *seem* rather than to *be*— and is on guard against the temptation to step into it. Therefore, he is characterized by candidness, expression, and genuinely being himself.

One illustration will make the point clear. A young clergyman was appointed to serve as minister to students on a state college campus in the South. With a group of students he was attending a revival service one evening in a local church. As part of the service the pastor of the church asked all the visiting ministers to stand, and when they were on their feet, he invited each of them to give a "testimony" of his conversion experience. Each in turn described the circumstances and time of his "experience." This young man had had no such experience in the traditional concept of the word—certainly not the kind of experience that could be nailed down as to time and place and circumstance. When his turn came, he endeared himself to many of the people present, though he caused consternation in many of the others (especially the pastor), by honestly confessing in a halting voice that he had

[6] Sidney M. Jourard, *The Transparent Self* (Princeton: D. Van Nostrand Co., 1964), p. 2.

had no such experience—that he was constantly being converted, constantly being changed, and, hopefully, constantly growing.

This does not discredit the experience being called for by the testimonial service. It is to emphasize the honesty of the young man and to point out that traditions may manipulate us into being dishonest about our religious experiences. Appreciation of differences is one of the hallmarks of actualization. We must recognize this in the conversion process as well as in other areas.

The young minister was not willing to hide behind the mask of words or the facade of a fictitious experience that he could not truly confess. This kind of honesty or authenticity characterizes the person who is seeking to be actualizing.

AWARENESS

The second characteristic of the actualizor is awareness. He is alive and responsive. He looks at and listens to himself and others. The real dimensions of living are vital in his life— whether these dimensions be in nature, in personal relationships, in art, in music, or in religion. As we seek to live the actualizing life, we come to understand more and more the meaning of Evelyn Underhill's affirmation: "God is always coming to you in the sacrament of the present moment. Meet and receive him then with gratitude in that sacrament, however unexpected its outward form may be."

This awareness incorporates a number of dimensions. There is knowledge, sensitivity, discernment, and appreciation. All these dimensions are related to oneself, to others, to the world, to events, and to God. It is obvious that this awareness is cultivated. While we are born with a basic inquisitiveness, that endowment soon dies unless developed. The actualizing person is aware of the responsibility that is his to gain knowledge, to grow in sensitivity, to practice discernment, to cultivate appreciation. In a world like ours, to be aware in this many-faceted way seems quite impossible. Bodies of knowledge are so vast, relationships are so impersonal, decisions are so complex, and all that calls forth appreciation is so endless that it would be quite defeating if we thought in terms of "oughtness." Awareness is not a command or a law; it is an opportunity or a privilege. What is called for here is not a superhuman person who knows, discerns, is sensitive to, and appreciative of all that is available, but one who sees life through wide-angle lenses and responds to life with a readiness to learn and an excitement to grow and share.

G. K. Chesterton once said of Omar Khayyám: "The trouble with the Persian poet is that he spent his whole life in the cellar and thought it the only room in the house." This is the prison from which the actualizing person has escaped. We know that the world and people consist of many rooms, and these rooms are variously decorated and variously furnished. We are alive in our interest to all these dimensions and know that they have something to contribute to our lives, and we have something to contribute to theirs.

FREEDOM

The third characteristic of an actualizing style of life is freedom. For the actualizing person this has not become the empty word that it is for some. It does not mean the absence from restraint or authority that it has been reduced to in some quarters. The freedom of the actualizor means spontaneity and openness. It means that the crutches of life are diminishing and the false supports on which we have so long depended in our manipulative living are no longer needed. We know that we are "thous" who are not puppets for manipulating or objects for controlling, but subjects for acting and responding, feeling and being. "Freedom of speech," said Dr. Robert M. Hutchins, "is empty unless we have something to say." Freedom for persons is meaningless unless we are on our way to becoming authentic persons—transparent persons—who communicate love, warmth, concern, and passion.

Freedom is really a spirit of, or stance toward, life. It has little or nothing to do with our circumstances. An old hymn expresses it,

> Our fathers, chained in prisons dark,
> Were still in heart and conscience free.

There is a sense in which the actualizing person to a great degree is the master of his life. This is no "master-of-my-fate, captain-of-my-soul" mastery, but the mastery that comes from recognizing and accepting one's varied potentials and expressing those potentials in the circumstances of the moment.

Maslow lists Lincoln among the great actualizors of history; he could prosecute the bloody war between the American states, but he could also weep at the death of a soldier boy. And what was it that kept him through those terrible years of the Civil War? He carried the weight of all the terrible choices when nobody seemed to know what to do.

Carl Sandburg, who devoted much of his life to a study of this man, gives us the secret. Addressing a group of young college men at a commencement exercise in the midst of another great war that brought confusion and bitterness, he said, "Young gentlemen, I think you need the spirit of prayer and humility of Abraham Lincoln who, in 'the divided house' of his day, knew what to do because he knew who he was." This is the freedom of the actualizing person. We usually know what to do because we know who we are; we remain steady and certain in the midst of confusion and uncertainty because of this self-knowledge, self-acceptance, and self-appreciation.

TRUST

The fourth characteristic of the actualizing person is trust. This is a deep trust in oneself and a willingness to relate and cope with life in the here and now. Without relationship there is no wholeness for man. While the manipulator is basically distrusting of himself and others and resorts to controlling and being controlled, the actualizor, deep down, trusts other humans and himself. Because of this basic trust, we enter into relationships.

Again we call on Martin Buber for insight. In a world which had become "thing-centered" and had lost its humanity, even placing God as a "thing" alongside other things, he pierced the confusion and began to speak of "thou," of "presence," of "meeting," and of "persons." Real life is *meeting*, he said. In the mutuality and directness of the present, man becomes truly a person in the "I-thou" relationship. This "I" cannot be an "I" without trust; and this "thou" cannot be a "thou" without trust. So the actualizing person has a deep trust in himself and others—so deep and basic that he is willing to risk real "meeting."

Trust, in the actualizing sense, is seen in its near-perfect state in little children who have *not yet learned* to be cynical

31

and distrustful in relationships. They exchange all sorts of possessions, accept each other's word, and believe what others say. There is a directness and a simplicity that is free of innuendoes, hidden agendas, and unspoken meaning. There is also the spontaneous expression of feelings, as the child is willing to trust himself and be himself in relationships.

Though very early the child learns distrust and becomes selfish, is often grabbing and fighting, there is a distinct difference between his trustful spontaneity and that of the adult. This is at least a part of what Jesus was talking about when he said, "Unless you become as a little child, you will not enter the kingdom."

Nelly Sachs, recipient of the Nobel Prize in Literature committed herself to this kind of trust and called for it from others in her acceptance of the prize at the Paulskirche in Frankfurt in October, 1965. She had been the victim of the Nazi rise to power and had witnessed all the "Houses of Death" that would normally lead to cynicism. Addressing the young German generation, she said, "In spite of all the horrors of the past, I believe in you. . . . Together, full of grief, let us remember the victims, and then let us walk together into the future to seek again and again a new beginning—maybe far away, yet ever-present; let us try to find the good dream that wants to be realized in our hearts." [7]

[7] Gertrude C. Schwebell, "Nelly Sachs," *The Saturday Review*, December 10, 1966, p. 47.

Chapter II
Manipulative Styles of Life

There is a song in the musical *South Pacific* that proclaims an obvious truth:

> You've got to be taught to hate . . .
> You've got to be carefully taught.[1]

Substitute the word "manipulate" for hate, and you have another truth.

All of us are carefully taught to manipulate. In this chapter we want to identify some manipulative patterns that are part of our common culture.

The key is style. All of us consciously and unconsciously are constantly involved in developing a style of life. Most of us can confess that the styles discussed here have influenced our lives, though we may not have adopted them fully. By *style* we mean the stance one takes in relation to the total experience of life.

[1] "You've Got to Be Carefully Taught." Copyright © 1949 by Richard Rodgers and Oscar Hammerstein II. Used by permission of Williamson Music, Inc.

A good illustration may be taken from boxing. Every boxer has a stance; he bends his knees in order to be mobile and elude his opponent. He crouches in order to minimize his vulnerability. He keeps his arms and fists in front of him, to protect himself and to be ready to strike offensively when the openings come. A boxer has a style that is identifiable. The purpose of this chapter is to outline some styles of life that have been popular and widely adopted. Their manipulative and thus self-defeating characteristics should be recognized.

The Middle-Class American Style: "The Good Life"

A common life-style sought out by many American men is "the good life." This is a general style, and from it a variety of similar styles come. Everyone who seeks "the good life" is not necessarily a blatant manipulator, but there can be significant manipulative patterns which characterize this search.

The "good-lifer" is one who is on the achievement tread-mill. He is so goal oriented that he fails to live meaningfully in the moment. As he pursues his goals, he becomes tomorrow oriented and has a great deal of trouble living in the here and now.

"The good life" will always be reached tomorrow when he achieves the "proper" status, attains the power that is not yet in his grasp, and accumulates the wealth that will take him to the top of the economic pyramid.

Because of his busyness the good-lifer has no time for his family. His weeks are filled with broken promises to his wife and children concerning the experiences that they want to share with him. He is the man who cannot take a vacation and buys any number of things that he never has time to use.

34

He is a doer, a compulsive pusher of himself and everyone around him.

The good-lifer works even at his play. His dream is the good life, but he discovers little of the reality of it. Often he rationalizes his poor relationships with his family and associates with a sort of martyr feeling, "I'm doing everything I can to see that they have the good life."

The good-lifer operates on the basis of "joy through success." He has to be achieving and winning the game even though his achievements and wins bring him only the most transitory satisfaction.

The assumption of the good-lifer, often incorrect, is that others around him share his idea of the good life. A couple who came for counseling shared their most troubled feelings about their relationship.

Wife: You work hard, but you control almost every purchase we make. You never trust me to decide on what we need around the home, and I feel just like your child who has to ask every time she wants a nickel for a popsicle.

Husband: But you know that I am just trying to make sure that we have enough to live on later. We have to sacrifice now to be secure in the future. I've been making us toe the line for us. Surely you know this.

Wife: Just when did we ever make this agreement? I'd like to live a little right now.

The good-lifer is often out of contact with his own inner feelings and personal needs, as well as out of contact with others. His goals often take precedence over his experiencing life in the here and now. Studies of persons whose careers demand a high degree of intellectual competence reveal that these persons as a group are, to a high degree, out of contact with their own feelings.

Ideas as to what defines the good life vary sharply in our society. To one it is the accumulation of status goods and the conspicuous consumption of approved articles. To another it is the mastery of the discipline of some specialized skill or body of knowledge. For another it is the ability to experience pleasure yet make no commitment. For another it is giving oneself to a cause.

Whatever the definition of the good life, the possibility of manipulation is always present if in the search for the good life we deny our innermost feelings, ignore the needs and capabilities of others, and refuse to take responsibility for our environmental situation.

The Hemingway Style: "You Only Live When You Are Close to Death"

This pervasive style of life is a continuing one in Western civilization, and from it many other styles grow.

A recent film had as its plot line the story of a man who was impotent sexually unless he was seducing someone and in danger of being caught by her lover, husband, brother, or fiancé. The hero of the film was only alive sexually and in other ways when he was in danger.

Perhaps the greatest spokesman for this style of life was the writer Ernest Hemingway. His books are full of characters who only reach fulfillment when they are in danger of dying. The most emphatic statement on this style of life can be found in Hemingway's continuing focus on the bullfighter as the man who lives life to the fullest. The moment of truth is the central thesis of this style of life and comes as the matador is poised over the horns of a bull, with sword ready for the kill. One is totally vulnerable in this kind of situation.

Hemingway's men *seek out* the dangerous experience. They place themselves in the jungle and pit their skill and courage against the elements and the beasts. In Hemingway's book *The Old Man and the Sea,* the fisherman chooses to keep his rendezvous with death. The struggle is not really with the fish; it is within the man.

For the followers of this style of life awareness is discovered in dangerous situations. Only when a person faces death does he reach an awareness of himself and the deeper meanings of life. Anyone who has had serious surgery or has faced the meaning of his own mortality in other situations knows that there is a great deal of validity in this assumption.

The manipulation in this style of life is revealed in the artificially contrived situations that men seek out in order to discover if they can make it through their moment of truth. When one picks out a dangerous spot in which to jump in order to discover himself, then he has manipulated by controlling the situation. Too often this life-close-to-death style results in role playing rather than real life involvement.

The source of this style may be found in one of the primary manipulative characteristics: *cynicism.* The man who must prove himself and who demands that every other man prove himself by defying death is basically *distrusting* of himself and others. He is not sure if he can measure up to the dangers of life. He is not certain that he will have the courage and power to cope with the situations of life that come naturally

37

to him. So he seeks out experiences like fighting an animal, or a man, or driving a racing car faster than anyone else, or climbing a mountain—experiences that few have had before. Because of a basic cynicism, the person is continually forced to reaffirm self-faith.

The life-close-to-death style of living is a style that leads to manipulation rather than to actualization. The central characteristic of actualization that is precluded by this style is that of *trust*. The man who must set up experiences to discover whether he is big enough to get through them is a man without trust in his ability to cope with life in the here and now. Though the man who puts himself in death-defying situations is admired and valued in our culture, he may be one of our biggest manipulators.

The Hippie Style: "Make Love Not War"

Numbers of young adults have responded to the suggestion of Dr. Timothy Leary, former professor at Harvard, to "tune in, turn on, and drop out." They are adopting a "hip" style of life.

This style is in such flux and so varied in expression that it is impossible to wrap into one tight little package. There are elements, however, that are common to large segments of the hippie subculture.

Unconventional dress is one hallmark of many hippies. Their lives seem to the outsider like one continuous costume party. Their goal is to be as highly individualized as possible. In some instances unconventional dress is related to unclean dress. Long hair is part of the style. Unconventional dress is related to reaction against mass society and mass styles.

Unconventional values are another part of the hippie style of life. One of the patron saints of the hippie movement is Henry David Thoreau, the recluse of Walden Pond, who rejected his own particular culture and constellation of values. Most hippies are not goal oriented in terms of achieving status or material goods. "Why should I waste my life working?" "What's so good about having a house and a color TV and a big car?" Many hippies are curiously passive and nonviolent in contrast to the violent society in which they live.

Unconventional community. For many of the hippies the only way to live is by a sort of nondogmatic communism. The hippie community is a community of share and share as much alike as possible. Hippie havens such as the Haight-Ashbury district in San Francisco are somewhat like communities of refugees who have been thrown together after some natural disaster. But even as this is being written, hippies are moving from Haight-Ashbury because tourists have "spoiled" it for them. Even so, hippieland exists in every main United States city and half a dozen foreign capitals. Its inhabitants may number as many as 250,000. They eat where they can, seeking handouts as needed—sleep where they can, sometimes moving often. Mutual dependence is the rule rather than the exception. The great desire of the hippie individual and the hippie community is to be together.

Unconventional sex. Sexuality for many hippies is the key part of their quest for freedom. Living together and sleeping around is not the style of all hippies, but enough of them participate to give the group the highest rate of venereal disease of any subculture in America. In some hippie groups the sharing of sex is considered just as important as the sharing of drugs. People have no right to withhold either. Sexual experiences are seen as being characterized by spontaneous gratification, rather than long-term commitment and responsibility of the sexual partners for each other.

Unconventional drugs. The hippie style of life includes unconventional drugs to provide peak experiences and to bring one to the point of heightened awareness. The hippie has grown up in the midst of a drug-centered culture (alcohol, tobacco, caffein, tranquilizers, pep pills), but these drugs fail to move him. His goal is mind expansion, not mind anesthetization—he wants to see visions and dream dreams, not see pink elephants and fall into a drunken sleep. So, the hippie takes nonconventional, illegal drugs.

Unconventional protest. The hippie style of life is basically a protest style of life. Since to the hippie any kind of aggression for personal gain is a kind of anathema, any kind of competitiveness or combativeness is a threat to the hippie style; and since the hippie is usually a person who has given up on "democratic" methods of change, the hippie protests in unconventional ways.

Art and music accentuate the hippie life-style. "Come to San Francisco" was a folk-rock tune which was one big advertisement for people to come to San Francisco to participate in the hippie community. "The Acapulco Gold" was a song which turned out to be an advertisement for a kind of "pot" to turn the listeners on. Hippie art is interpretive, with an often intricate code which accents the insulation of the hippie style from the "square."

The hippie style of life is a style that is reaching toward actualization. Manipulation is still present. Hippies are the great *users* of what they consider incidental. They are participants in a giant throw-away of what they consider to be a disposable society.

Although love is the watchword of the hippie, it seems to be a rare experience. An amorphous sort of love in general is proclaimed and practiced in lieu of any *one-to-one* continuing relationships which are characterized by caring and long-term commitment. Short-term spontaneous happenings, covered over with the word "love," still spell out manipulation in terms of exploitation sexually and psychologically.

Hippies, in many cases, seem to be persons who have extreme problems with love. Self-hate leads them to degrade themselves and toss away even their sanity in a desperate attempt to discover meaning. Their manipulation of life with drugs perhaps stems from the lack of any meaningful relationships with persons older than themselves. This lack of meaningful relationships manifests itself in hostile cynicism.

Though it is rarely a violent hostility, it runs deep enough to cause the hippie to conceive of, if not treat, non hippies with a superior scorn. Perhaps this is a reaction to the scorn which the hippie faces, but it results in a gulf between the hippie and those who are not yet "enlightened" or "turned on."

Passive manipulation is also inherent in the hippie style. Though he "judges" society and "drops out," the hippie remains dependent upon the establishment he has denounced.

The pervasiveness of this style of life is only slowly dawning on the collective consciousness of America. Whatever the hippie is and wherever he is going, it cannot be denied that it is our society that has produced him. There may have been hippie-like people in all ages of our society—people who heard the beat of another drum and marched off in another direction from the conventional populace. But we have never had such a large hip community before. It has become a society within a society, with its own unwritten laws, its own symbolism.

The Playboy Style: "Wine, Women and Song"

One of the most popular styles of life for young adults is presented in one of the fastest-selling monthly magazines on the stand, *Playboy*. It defines values and a life-style for millions of young men. Its pages contain advice on goals, and its writers attempt to dictate choices and govern the decisions of its readership. So prominent is this style of life that popular author John D. MacDonald, through his fictional character Travis McGee, has to show his awareness of it, though he dismisses it with a casual contempt that must be irritating to Hugh Hefner, father of the style.

I do not know why anyone should expect anything special from a place where the Hefner empire seems to represent some sort of acme of sophistication, based as it is upon fantastic centerfold mammalian for the pimpled self-lovers, upon a chain of bunny-warrens styled to make the middle-class sales manager feel like a member of the in-group, and upon a laborious philosophical discourse which runs interminably in the ad-happy magazine and in the polysyllabic style of the pseudo-educationed, carrying the deathless message that it is healthy to screw and run if everybody is terribly sincere about it.[2]

Playboy presents for its readers each month complete directions on life. The editor, Hugh Hefner, has spelled out over a number of issues his complete philosophy of the *Playboy* life. An outgrowth of this style has been the establishment of *Playboy* clubs where members may practice this life-style with other devotees of the *Playboy* philosophy.

This philosophy defines heaven as a place on earth where

[2] *One Fearful Eye* (New York: Fawcett Books, 1966), p. 45.

one has all the right things. To be a part of this life one must achieve and exhibit the approved articles of consumption. The playboy will have the right kind of "pad," the right kind of sports car, wear the right kind of clothes, and be seen in the right kind of places.

Besides the obvious consumption of things, the *Playboy* style includes the conspicuous consumption of persons. The *Playboy* philosophy teaches young men how to relate to women. The center of attraction each month is the play-mate of the month, always a beautiful young woman attired scantily or wearing nothing in a photograph foldout page in the middle of the magazine.

Playboy "bunnies" are the hostesses in the *Playboy* clubs. Their job is to be available to the playboy. The *Playboy* bunny is to stimulate the playboy's desires but to never fulfill them. The management of the *Playboy* clubs has set up strict rules for the conduct of bunnies. They may not touch one of the customers or be touched by them. They may not have a cus-tomer escort them home from the club. In this style of life looking is permitted, but nothing further—at least on the premises of the *Playboy* club. This encourages a form of voyeurism.

One of the central premises of this style of life is that the fulfilled life is the sex-filled life. Handy hints on how to im-press and seduce a girl are spelled out in sophisticated ways. One of the ten commandments for young men in this style of life could be "Thou shalt not get married." The moment a man marries, he loses his playboy status.

Sexual enjoyment without involvement or responsibility for the sexual partner's life is a chief cornerstone. Some parts of the *Playboy* philosophy reveal a reaction to restrictions on or *use* of people found in moral codes and teachings of the church. "We do not consider sex either sacred or profane. The nonsense about the body being evil and the spirit good seems preposterous to most of us today. A guilty feeling persists that there is something evil in the flesh of man. This is a carry-over from the Puritanism of our fathers," writes Hugh Hefner.

The manipulations of this style of life at its worst run through the characteristics of deception, control, and cynicism. The manipulative playboy spends his time trying to create an impression by buying the prescribed elements of the *Playboy* life-style. In some cases, he is encouraged to control his relationships by concealing his motives from the young women to whom he relates. His final goal is enjoyment without responsibility. So the woman becomes a thing to be used, not a person to be appreciated. Like his sports car, his hi-fi, and his pad, a woman becomes an accessory—a possession to enhance his image.

The *Playboy* philosophy vigorously denies this. It contends that women are grateful to enter into playboy relationships. The emphasis is on mutual sexual enjoyment of playboys and bunnies in a consenting adult relationship. The reality of the situation is that even the playboy has difficulty finding women who want sex without a personal commitment.

The policy of the magazine is to develop the image that young women want to live free of continuing relationships and seek out the symbols of the playboy and the playboy himself for their fulfillment. The magazine itself has great difficulty in discovering young women who follow this style of life. We know personally a young woman who appeared as a playmate of the month. The article, which included a number of

44

pictures of her, stated that she was single, loved to date play-boy men, lived in a luxurious pad, and sailed on a yacht. The truth is, this woman was married, lived in a modest apart-ment, and had never been on a yacht before the pictures of her were taken. Her primary interest in *Playboy* was the lucrative fee received for her photograph. The *Playboy* style of life is manipulative in that it is *body centered* rather than *person centered*. It encourages "it-it" rather than "thou-thou" relationships.

The Cosmo Style: "Arsenal of Sex"

The inversion of the *Playboy* style of life for men is what Allen J. Moore has termed the "cosmo girl." The manipu-lations of the playboy are centered on the goal of eluding mar-riage and commitment. The manipulations of the cosmo girl are focused on the opposite goal. Marriage is her aim.

The cosmo girl is the life-style that is outlined in *Cosmo-politan* magazine. This magazine is now under the direction of Helen Gurley Brown, the author of *Sex and the Single Girl*. *Sex and the Single Girl* was written around such ques-tions as: "How does a girl go about having an affair?" "How does she clear the decks for action?" "What is the best place for her to consummate the affair?" Mrs. Brown stated that a big part of the single girl's "arsenal of sex" is her apartment, her clothes, and the fact that she can give an intimate little dinner. A full-page ad was taken in the *New York Times* to point out the "happy rewarding life" of the new "Cosmopoli-tan Girl." Since Mrs. Brown has taken over, *Cosmopolitan* has become one of the favorite magazines for the unmarried urban woman.

At first appearance the cosmo girl resembles the fantasy of

Playboy's playmate. She is sexually free, uninhibited, fun-loving, and most of all desirable. "Taking a page out of the *Playboy's* philosophy and turning it around, the Cosmo girl sees man as an object, an accessory to play with (meaning, to manipulate). With luck, she can turn him ultimately into guaranteed security." [3]

Things and sex are the hallmarks of this style of life. For the cosmo girl, sex is seen as a weapon to manipulate man into giving her what she wants. The weapon of the playboy male is that he knows all the right places to go, has all the correct (wish-fulfillment) apparatus, and knows all of the right things to do.

The truth of the matter is, *Cosmopolitan* has turned the tables on the male magazines and has taken sex as its chief commodity. Sexual references, sexual symbols, and sexology are not everything in the magazine, but are certainly the dominant themes of each issue. . . . Features have dealt with male impotence, ground rules for office affairs, nightwear to "make you the only entertainment a man could want after his day's work," guide to the best male lovers, . . . and hints on "how to write love letters." [4]

The single young adult female is provided with an identity in the pages of *Cosmopolitan* as is her counterpart in the pages of *Playboy*. The manipulation of the cosmo style of life is the further depersonalization of sex. The cosmo style sees sex as a technique to achieve a goal, not as an end in itself. The result of the cosmo style of life is the dehumanizing and desacralizing of sex. Both the *Playboy* and the Cosmo

[3] Allen J. Moore, "The Cosmo Girl," *Christian Advocate*, January 12, 1967, p. 7.
[4] *Ibid.*

styles of life can lead to the deceptive and cynical patterns that make up the characteristics of the manipulator.

The emphasis is placed on the attainment of desirability, not in the sharing of total selfhood.

The James Bond Style: "Dames, Death, and Destruction"

One pattern or style of life that has become international in scope in the past few years is the James Bond style. James Bond is Agent 007, the mythical man of Ian Fleming's fiction.

The image of the James Bond life-style hit the culture of America with a hurricane force in the 60's. Millions went to sleep with his rugged, deadly, life-lived-to-the-hilt adventures sending them vicariously into battles with absolutely evil men and sexual relationships with absolutely beautiful women. Over 45 million copies of the James Bond books have been sold, and more than 100 million persons have attended the James Bond films. This style of life has had wide exposure!

The James Bond style is at first glance the style of a modern knight in a finely tailored suit—a personification of competence (James Bond is an expert marksman, mechanic, gourmet, wit, conversationalist, lover) and always on the side of right and justice. His style is seen by some as the style of a modern St. George who sets out to slay the dragons of the twentieth-century world.

A careful analysis of the completed work reveals it as a saga of a modern knight whose adventures involve a gallery of modern demons which have been attacking contemporary mankind just as diabolically as Medusa and all the other legendary demons and dragons attacked mankind in ages past. Rather than casting pearls before swine, Fleming's genius has cast swine as the personification of the devil before a hero who is willing to sacrifice all for the great pearl of life and faith.[5]

This style of life has had its most direct effect upon the adolescents who are seeking a hero figure and are searching for values. It cuts through the boredom of many of their lives with titillating promise of escape from meaninglessness. James Bond is a hero figure in a world of broken images. He is a replacement for life-styles that have been tried and found wanting.

In many of his relationships Bond is the master manipulator. His out is that he is always seeking to manipulate for just causes. Bond lives in a world of objects. He is incapable of lasting relationships because he has discovered that he can trust no one. The hallmark of manipulative relationships is distrust.

In his struggles against manipulation he becomes a manipulator. He outmanipulates the great evil manipulators. His is a solitary life with only episodic encounters with other persons. His style is to live precariously and anonymously. His patterns are summed up in the ballad that precedes the television show *Secret Agent*.

> There's a man who leads a life of danger,
> To everyone he meets he stays a stranger,
> With every move he makes
> Another chance he takes.
> Odds are, he won't live to see tomorrow.

[5] Ann S. Boyd, *The Devil with James Bond* (Richmond: John Knox Press, 1966), p. 29.

48

Secret agent man, secret agent man—
They've given you a number—
And taken away your name![6]

In the relationship with women the Bond style is to remain a stranger. The closeness is all physical closeness. As in the *Playboy* style, sex is sex without love. In Bond's sexual relationships he manipulates and is often manipulated. Evil comes in the form of a voluptuous woman, as it did in the person of Pussy Galore in the film *Goldfinger*. Although unalterably opposed in terms of commitment to values and institutions, James Bond and Pussy Galore have no problem entering into the most intimate relationship of all: sexual intercourse.

The Bond style uses persons as though they were things. Love is never a part of this style. Integrity for the Bond style is limited to destruction of the enemy. Efficiency in destroying the enemy is the first virtue. Bond's only prized possession is a favorite weapon. He uses his body as a tool, armed with judo and karate.

Mechanical manipulation also plays a role. Nothing is spared to equip Bond with all the latest gadgets of manipulation and destruction, so we find him using supersensitive "bugging" devices, cars with smoke-screen capability, machine guns under the headlights, and ejection seats for the elimination of an enemy.

"To everyone he meets he stays a stranger." That is the key to the danger in the Bond style. He never loves and is never loved. No one loves him! Women desire him, give

[6] The words of the song "Secret Agent Man" by P. F. Sloan and Steve Barri are © Copyright 1965 by Trousdale Music Publishers, Inc., 1330 Avenue of the Americas, New York, N. Y. 10019. All rights reserved. Used by permission.

themselves to him, but never really love him. No one knows Bond. He is presented as the *aware* man (a characteristic of actualization). But Bond's awareness is not actualizing. Aware of the soft spots of the human species, he makes his world the world of manipulative cynicism. His self can never be known. He must spend his days bravely defying death, destruction, and dames by putting himself against the mad enemies who abound. No one can be trusted.

To be truly human and actualizing is to love and be loved. Actualizors enter into long-term relationships. Bond has none. In Fleming's first novel, *Casino Royale*, Bond is told by his boss not to become human.

Now that you have seen a truly evil man you will know how evil they can be, and you will go after them to destroy them in order to protect yourself and the people you love. You won't wait or argue about it. You know what they look like now and what they can do to people. You may be a bit more choosey about the jobs you take on. You may want to be certain that the target is really black. . . . Surround yourself with human beings, my dear James. They are easier to fight for than principles. . . . But don't let me down and become human yourself. We would lose such a wonderful machine.[7]

Since the Bond style of life succeeds in being more machine-like than human-like, it must be rejected as characteristically manipulative.

The Drug Style: "Tune in, Turn on, Drop Out"

A style of life that has had popularity in our time includes taking so-called "mind-expanding" drugs. The most

[7] (New York: The Macmillan Company, 1953), p. 112.

widespread drug is lysergic acid, better known as LSD. While this style originally attracted principally teen-agers and young adults, it is now spreading into other groups.

The stated goal of this style of life is the attainment of one of the prime characteristics of actualization: *awareness*. The takers of LSD and like drugs claim to be involved in a process of fully looking at themselves and others. The LSD user makes life experience centered. The terminology of this style includes "taking a trip," "flying," and "tuning in."

Styles of life may take on some of the characteristics of a religious movement. The LSD style has its prophets and martyrs—professors who have become devotees of the drug and have lost their positions. According to the followers of the movement, they have been persecuted by the law. There are "sacred writings" which are closely followed to set the doctrine and practice of the new religion. These are the books written or edited by the highly regarded leaders. *The Psychedelic Experience* (a manual based on the Tibetan Book of the Dead), by Timothy Leary, Ralph Metzner, and Richard Alpert, is an example.

Like many other religious styles the LSD style claims absolute results for those who will join the ranks. This style promises that the drugs, as the sacramental means of grace, will enable the taker to understand himself in a new way and lead him into a deeper awareness of what life is all about.

The followers of this drug-centered style of life become very evangelistic and fervent in their attempt to make converts. Witness some of the statements of one of the leaders, Dr. Timothy Leary, psychologist and former instructor at Harvard: "We are starting a new religious revival: We are calling people to tune in, turn on, and drop out"; we intend

51

to put psychiatry out of business." A "Group LSD" pamphlet advertised the drug experience as "a safe and successful program for the solving of human problems and the transformation of life," and told of five hundred outcasts of society, "the rejected fringe of humanity," whose lives were transformed.

The object of this style is to produce *psychedelic celebrations*. "We are going to turn on America, then Europe, then Asia." Attempts are made to heighten the awareness of persons participating in the drug experience through the use of art and more traditional religious resources.

The use of drugs to produce actualization may be a valid resource in the future. At this time, however, the overwhelming majority of scientists and trained observers of personality patterns reject the use of drugs as being dangerous. In many cases the taking of LSD and other like drugs is certainly manipulative and harmful, rather than providing the desired results of actualization.

The manipulative characteristic most pronounced in LSD takers is *unawareness*. Studies of large numbers of persons who have come into the hospitals for treatment reveal a feeling of deadness and boredom in many who have chosen this style of life. "That beautiful young woman sitting in the corner," said a doctor in Los Angeles County Hospital, "believes that she is an orange. She has been noncommunicative for days. She will not respond to any human contact." The drug style of life is one way of reaching detachment from the struggles of the world. In many ways it parallels the thinking of some Eastern cults in its sense of negativeness about life.

This style of life becomes manipulative with the cynical

view that the fulfilled life is reached only by understanding that one can do nothing about the outside world. It encourages its followers not to change things but only to go deeper into oneself. Manipulation of the mind through the use of drugs is not new. What is new is the widespread use and acceptance of these new drugs in our culture.

The Supremist Style: "Ours Is the True Way"

The supremist style of life is characterized by an absolute belief in the rightness of one's views or the purposes of one's institution or system. Only absolute loyalty and obedience will do for the supremist. In this style no criticism or departure from the status quo is permitted. Any deviation from the stated order of the pronounced articles of faith is seen by the supremist as being traitorous.

The supremist is often a person who uses all the tactics of manipulation to save himself and others from manipulation that is real or imagined. In this instance the supremist fits most closely the role of the *protector* in the theory of *Man, the Manipulator*. The person who practices this style claims that he does what he does because he doesn't want to see people get hurt.

The supremist is often found claiming that he is the holder of the absolute truth in such areas of life as religion, race, and politics. The supremist exaggerates his "top-dog" potentials—that is, his strength—because he is basically insecure and incomplete. Thus, he also may be described as a dictator-manipulator type. He cannot generate self-assurance out of his rejected self, so finds it only by clinging blindly to whatever support he happens to embrace. This passionate attachment is felt to be the source of all virture and strength. Even though his fanatical dedication is seen by him as loyal and devoted support to a holy cause, it is in reality a frantic effort to prove his worth.

This style is dependent on a "devil" theory of history. The supremist always needs a well-defined enemy to do battle with. The enemy can be "the mongrelizers of the races," "the Comsymps," "the left-wingers," "the apostates," "the heretics," or any number of other "devil" characters. Someone or something that is threatening his way of life is necessary, even if it must be created. The supremist often claims that he is the true patriot and the only one who is really loyal. He boasts powers of prophecy and inside information on what will take place in the near future. His attitude is that of a misunderstood martyr: "No one else is paying any attention to this great danger and evil, but I will be loyal."

One main focus of this style is the method of manipulating by projecting. The supremist manipulator transfers his feelings onto other persons and groups or even mythical situations. T. W. Adorno in the famous work, *The Authoritarian Personality,* describes how the German people, unable to accept their own sexual and acquisitive desires, projected them onto the Jews and then punished the group on which they had projected them. The supremist pushes his unwanted feelings off onto others. This attitude is related to the collective myth of many white persons concerning Negroes. The Negro race in America has become the great dumping ground for the unacceptable and unresolved sexual and economic feelings and relationships of the whites. John Dollard also maintains that the popular images of the Negro as lazy, virile, and sexually promiscuous are at base the projected unacceptable feelings of the whites.[8]

Wherever supremacy manipulation is widespread, the continuous projected images produce the self-fulfilling prophecy. The manipulated persons find it difficult to develop identity-images other than those given them by the power structure in a controlled society. Members of minorities have become aware of this and are trying to remedy the situation by working for a more balanced interpretation of history in textbooks.

The supremist works to deaden awareness and to keep his victims in a childlike state of dependence. The policy of the Belgian government in relation to their colony of the Congo is a case in point. For many years the Belgian policy was to give the citizens of the Congo only a minimum level of education because "they were not ready." When independence was finally granted because of immense internal and external pressure in 1960, there were only six Congolese college graduates out of 16 million persons!

When persons are given no other identity-images or styles to pattern their lives after, they tend to enact the expectation of others. This, in turn, enforces the prejudice. This is dramatically portrayed in *Andorra*, a play by Max Frisch. The central character of this play is thought by the residents of a town to be a Jewish foundling. In actuality he is the illegitimate gentile son of one of the town's residents. Through the suggestions of the townspeople he assumes more and more "Jewish" characteristics. He takes on or introjects the role expectations of the manipulative supremist until he has become a "Jew."

[8] John Dollard, *Caste and Class in a Southern Town* (Garden City, N. Y.: Doubleday & Co., 1957).

Harvey Cox points out the place of the supremist manipulator in *The Secular City*: "Cultures concentrate repressed feelings into roles which are forced on given individuals who in turn enact them." This type of role-expectation-manipulation by supremists can be seen in the life-style of persons in the Salem witch trials and in the "brainwashing" of American soldiers in the Korean War.

The supremist manipulator is cynical, believing that others are always trying to manipulate his life and that the only answer is to outmanipulate the manipulators. The supremist is found in many categories: racist, fanatic nationalist, super-patriot, bigoted religionist. The supremist misses the richness of polarities and lacks awareness of his power and the power of others to actualize.

The supremist would be completely confused by the statement of Adlai Stevenson, an actualizing person: "The real patriots are those who love America as she is but want the beloved to be more lovable. This is not treachery. This, as every parent, every teacher, every friend must know, is the truest and noblest affection."

The Black Muslim Style: "Radical Reaction to Oppression"

One rising style of life in America is limited to the Negro racial group. This is the life-style of the Black Muslim. This style of life is a complete way of existence for numbers of persons.

The Black Muslim style is religious and cultural at base. It affords its adherents a sense of pride and belonging. This style is based on a reaction to the years of inequality and injustice suffered by the Negro people in America, a disillusionment with the "Christian" style of life, and total despair of the Negro's ever achieving the "American" way of life.

Among the tenets of this style of life is the belief that the Negro race is superior to the white race and that all white people are devils. The statement of one of the leaders of this style, Malcolm X, upon hearing of an airplane crash in which 129 Southern white persons lost their lives, was, "That's good, God willed it that way. He's punishing all the white devils for the way they have treated the black man."

The followers of the Black Muslim style of life are highly jealous and evangelical. They seek converts with a radical determination. Among the most successful recruiting spots are prisons and other such institutions. Those seeking to follow this style of life are asked to give up drinking and smoking. There is also a strict code regarding dress—especially for women. The absolute leader of the Black Muslim movement, Elijah Mohammed, is considered a prophet by his followers and rules in autocratic fashion.

Among the things that followers of this style of life are not requested to give up is the use of weapons. This style is definitely not nonviolent and many of the members of the movement become part of an elite fighting and protective society called the fruit of Islam.

Like the white segregationist, this style seeks separation of the races and wishes to set up a society of its own. Integration between the races is forbidden.

The Style of the Disadvantaged: "Black Power"

Closely related to the Black Muslim style of life is the black power style. The most articulate spokesman and model for this style has been Stokely Carmichael, the former head of SNCC (Student Nonviolent Coordinating Committee).

This style of life is based on the assumption that the black man must achieve political and economic power before he can have equality. This style of life looks upon the entire system of social and political apparatus of the United States as corrupt and unjust.

The followers of the black power style mean just what their slogan says—they mean to have power for black people. This style, like the style of the Black Muslim, stems from long-unmet, justifiable aspirations for freedom and dignity. It is a reaction to the manipulation used during slavery and, later, by discriminating white America.

The black power style would unite people along the lines of race to develop a bloc of power that will make a difference in government. This style is committed to restructuring the entire political and social system of the country. It is a style of life that determines both identity and goals for its adherents. Like any essentially religious style it demands obedience and sacrifice on the part of its followers.

Both the Black Muslim and some black power style advocates assume many manipulative characteristics. These styles attempt to turn the manipulative tables, seeking to have the roles reversed. Inasmuch as the Negro has been under-dog for so long, these styles promise him the possibility of becoming top-dog and lording it over the white man who has been the top-dog for too long.

The manipulative devices of criticalness, aggression, dictator strength, and calculating control are emphasized out of proportion to achieve the goals of mastery and separateness.

Such styles do provide a missing ingredient in many lives —identity, purpose, and hope. They have been developed out

58

of hopelessness and a wretched despair over other styles that seem to be shattered and broken for large numbers of persons.

The belief that America is the land of the free, a place where any man may rise up if he works hard enough and where each man is given the same rights and justice, is a cruel fantasy to many persons. Experience says "no" to this belief in the lives of millions. They know what it is to be divested of their freedom and dignity both by persons in control and by an impersonal system. They know the hell of manipulation. It is no wonder they wish to exchange their role of the manipulated for the role of the manipulator. But changing places will not produce actualization.

Chapter III
Manipulation in the Church

If man is a many-splendored composite of opposites, a congregation is a many-splendored organization of opposites. Take everything that is true about individual man and multiply it many times, and you have the congregation in all its complexity. Since manipulation has become the *modus operandi* of our culture, the church has not escaped being taken in by this style of life.

Manipulation in the Congregation

Any sensitive minister or layman is aware of the retreat to manipulation as a *modus operandi* of the local congregation. This is the kind of thing we talk about with tongue in cheek—if we talk about it at all. Sometimes we are prone to think that our dirty linen ought to be kept in the closet and not displayed for everyone to see. What happens as a result is that we really fail to face up to our manipulative practices, and the style of the congregation often becomes the style of manipulation. Congregational members manipulate each other. They manipulate the minister, and he manipulates them.

The following discussion is not exhaustive. It simply lists the practical devices, familiar to us all, that a congregation may use in manipulation. While the case is presented in the extreme, hopefully, it will cause us to at least take a look at the relationships within our churches to see where we are.

Cancel the pledge. Perhaps the most glaring manipulation is attempted through the financial structure of the church. Many otherwise thoughtful and sensitive laymen readily seek to control the ministry and mission of the church through the gifts they make. This is the first of the "ropes that choke."

During the tense days following the passage of the school desegregation law in 1954, some churches in the South began to venture more boldly into involvement in race relations. Ministers became a bit more courageous in their preaching. In several areas lay groups were organized in opposition to the church's involvement in such controversial matters. Organizations like the Mississippi Association of Methodist Ministers and Laymen fostered the idea that those who were opposed to such church involvement in public issues should withhold all contributions. In public statements they proclaimed that the only way to control the church was to control the purse strings. Young ministers who signed a "born-of-conviction" statement opposing racial discrimination in Mississippi were told by the church hierarchy that they cost the church $150,000 in gifts to benevolences. Newspaper accounts indicated that when Bishop James A. Pike of the Episcopal Diocese of California took his stand on Proposition 14 in 1964, large financial pledges of wealthy laymen across the state were cancelled.

If you can't control the church and its ministry any other way, "cancel the pledge!" So go the manipulator cries.

Cut off attendance. Another rope that chokes the local congregation is a passive manipulative device—withdrawal from participation. Many people seek to manipulate the direction of a local congregation by their presence or absence. If the direction is to their liking, they indicate it by their presence in the activities and worship of the church; if not to their liking, by their absence.

Coerce through committees: In many local congregations, according to the organizational structure, the minister and the entire congregation can be coerced through committees. Racists in Southern churches were urged to attend Quarterly Conferences of local Methodist churches to which they belonged and nominate from the floor people of like-mindedness for particular positions in the church where power could be exerted.

Create dissension. In all of life and certainly in the church people have learned that the creation of dissension among participants is a primary way of control. When there is enough dissension to be disruptive and divisive, ministers can be moved, programs altered, the emphasis shifted—the manipulator can move in to calm the troubled waters and settle the waves so that the tide may flow in the direction of his desires. He becomes the *protector* of the institution. Few, if any, of us have not been victims of the primary weapon of this technique: gossip. A word with multiple meaning is dropped here, an innuendo there, until an entire congregation (especially if it is a small one) is buzzing. It isn't unusual for the buzzing to become an uproar, and the manipulative "protector" can then do his work.

Cover up with clichés. In no place is the cliché more common than in the church. "I'd like to get back to good old-fashioned religion." "Preacher, why don't you just preach the Bible!" "Politics and religion just don't mix." "We've never done it this way before." On and on, *ad infinitum.* The use of these to confuse the issue and manipulate is common. Many vital considerations are never faced in congregations because they get lost in the cloudland of clichés.

Control the curriculum. The favorite sport of many within the church is the "control-the-curriculum game." Often the primary instrument used in this game is the Bible. "Just as long as we stick to the Bible in our studies!" Well, who can effectively argue against that? The effort here is deliberate and specific. No contemporary or controversial issues are faced. No contrary views are considered. Children, youth, and adults are fed a predigested pablum and are never given the opportunity to wrestle with issues or to have the freedom to make personal decisions.

Close the mind: Closing the mind is a passive manipulative technique used by many in the congregation. They simply will not listen. Harry Stack Sullivan says that one tends to become "selectively inattentive" to anything which threatens his sense of security. Many use this as a habitual pattern of behavior in order to cut off any idea that will threaten preconceived notions and prearranged prejudices. A minister may preach for years on the Christian principle of brotherhood, and nothing happens. Then he gets specifically involved in action that seeks to build brotherhood, and the fury of the congregation is brought down upon him. He may have been saying all the things he is now acting out, but people refused to hear or failed to understand. They closed their minds and became selectively inattentive.

Manipulating the minister. In how many ways does a congregation manipulate a minister! They idolize and tantalize. They make of him an "image" of purity and perfection and dare him to mar that image. They seduce him through gratuities such as country club memberships and ministerial discounts. Though gifts are given with no strings attached, people consciously and unconsciously get him in their debt.

In subtle ways people work to control the public opinions and proclamations of the minister. When contrary opinion or action is expressed, there is the unspoken "How can you do this to us?" and the "After all that we have done for you and now you embarrass us by your unpopular stand." This is the same technique used by the parent with his child. The implication is, if one loves another, then he can expect no opposition from the loved one. This ceases to be love and becomes a manipulative device of control.

The congregation sometimes "gets at" the minister through his wife and children. By casual remarks they convey points of concern. They resort to the fear technique by communicating to the wife information that they want to get to her husband. "I know you'd want to know this, and I'm sure you'll know how to break it to your husband. I'm concerned because of our friendship. A number of people are upset with your husband. He is certainly losing influence with a lot of people I know. His position in this matter is such an irritating and embarrassing one. If he just wouldn't be so insistent, I'm sure they would continue to accept him. But otherwise, I don't know what's going to happen." The word gets to its intended destination!

Both the wife and children of a minister desperately need the social relationships found in the community. However, these relationships are often controlled by the community in its attempt to control the minister. And the minister often falls into the snare. To protect his image he resorts to the manipulation of his family. By different techniques—conscious and unconscious—he coerces his family to conform to community standards. "What will the community think?" is a common question in a parsonage family. Those dearest to the minister are often forced to conclude that they are extensions of his pastoral prestige and ministerial ego.

Often a minister is manipulated into the pattern of "professional friend." Almost from the outset this style is forced upon him—he becomes the "hail-fellow, well-met." William E. Hulme reminds us that in Shepherd Mead's spoof of the future, *The Big Ball of Wax,* the leading ecclesiastical denomination is called "your church." Instead of being titled "reverend" or "father," the clergy of "your church" are addressed as "friendly." The founder of "your church" is the "Right Friendly Harry Wilkes Murray," who, as one might suspect, had previously been a top merchandising man.

For the minister who is excessively friendly and an accomplished promoter, success in the church is guaranteed. Here is two-way manipulation. The minister is manipulated into this position and finds that it works so well that he often deliberately follows the pattern and seeks to perfect it. In a marketplace culture this image is effective for the influence and control of people. The minister becomes the "nice guy."

So the ropes continue to choke. Until we can be free from them, the congregation will never function as God's people.

65

The Manipulating Minister

A manipulator may be defined as a person who maneuvers, uses, and/or controls himself and others as things or objects. He may be dressed in a clerical collar. He may use his clerics as an instrument of manipulation. The position he holds in the community, the way he comes to that position, and the leadership he exercises over a particular congregation place him in a unique situation for manipulation.

Rare is the minister who is not a manipulator to some degree. Rare, indeed, is the minister who is not the victim of manipulation. Heinrich Vogel was right when he said that in choosing the ministry, "one chooses to man an outpost of unequaled danger which threatens not only from without, but also from within."

Ministers are commonly seen as authority figures. Whether this is in keeping with the minister's desires or not doesn't matter. The very nature of his office sets him apart in this way. This image sets the stage for all the manipulative processes to spring into action. It is easy for him to play the *top-dog:* the bully, the judge, the dictator, or the calculator. Likewise, he can play the *under-dog:* the nice guy, the clinging vine, the weakling, or the protector. Consciously or unconsciously he plays the game that has been prescribed for him. Whether or not he plays by the rules is another question!

Even when the minister is not manipulative, people may feel manipulated because of his image of authority. An actualizing minister is aware of the false image of him that has been perpetuated and by his life-style—by open and democratic relationships—seeks to destroy it. In the minister's presence many people act differently than they normally do. The minis-

66

ter goes into the barber shop, and the language changes. The smutty stories are broken off, and a restrictive pall falls over the conversation.

The fact that many view the minister as a hired "professional Christian" doesn't help the problem. A double standard is set, and ministers are restricted in ways that are not applied to laymen. The rules against smoking and drinking, set by some denominations for ministers, but not applied to laymen, illustrate this. It is as though the minister is paid by the laymen to abstain from certain vices that they themselves will not forego.

Put thus in a position of being "other than" the layman, the minister finds the temptation to manipulate in the area of spiritual and moral authority irresistible. Since, for the manipulator, the understanding of human nature is for just one purpose—*control*—the minister too often fits the pattern and plays the game. Wielding his authority (in image and in fact), he controls those around him.

There are common ways that this is done, so common that we chuckle at the thought of them. But it's a nervous chuckle, for few, if any, will not identify with some of these manipulative devices.

The power of his profession. The manipulative minister feels that there are two types of Christians—the full-time ones and the part-time ones. As a full-time Christian (professional), he pulls rank and expresses his superiority by reference to the uniqueness of his call.

The *active* and the *passive* manipulators emerge here. The active manipulator continually reminds his congregation of the power of his profession and the authority vested in him as one "called of God." He seeks either directly or indirectly to create an aura of holiness around the ministerial office. His final authority is not in his person, but in his profession. When in conflict on an issue, he resorts to proclaiming himself on the Lord's side. And who will question the Word of God? He escapes intellectual conflict by resting his case on the revelation of God which comes to him and not to the unordained.

The passive manipulator who uses his profession as a manipulative device plays the role of the "humble servant of God" who takes his orders from above and is sorry that this role is in conflict with the opinions and ideas of others. He emphasizes his position as an under-dog in the community and thus manipulates people into following him.

The weight of his authority. When leading worship, preaching, administering the sacraments, officiating at services such as weddings and funerals, ministers are seen as vehicles of God's grace. It is so easy to manipulate by sharing or withholding grace.

A classic example of this was John Wesley's relation to Sophia Hopkey Williamson. As the only ordained minister in the Savannah colony, he was the spiritual authority. He used this authority and withheld the sacrament of Holy Communion from Sophia, whose affections he had sought to capture and whom, according to many, he had hoped to marry. Wesley gave as reasons for this refusal Sophia's failure to signify on the day before her intentions to partake of the Holy Communion and her refusal to openly declare herself in her sin, thus showing herself "to have truly repented." To her he wrote: "If you offer yourself at the Lord's Table on Sunday, I will advertise you (as I have done more than once) wherein you have done wrong. And when you have openly declared yourself to have truly repented, I will administer to you the mysteries of God."

Mr. Causton, uncle of Sophia and chief magistrate of Savannah, declared that "Mr. Wesley had repelled Sophia from the Holy Communion, purely out of revenge; because he had made proposals of marriage to her, which she rejected, and married Mr. Williamson."

Though Wesley denied this specific charge, he never denied his relationship to Sophia, and it is felt that a part of his misery in Georgia was due to her spurning his affection. Whether he actually denied her Holy Communion for this reason will remain a mystery, but the case illustrates the point. It *is* true that Wesley was soon on a ship returning to England without having earned the respect and trust of the people in the colony.

Often a minister will control his people by letting them know he feels that they are unworthy of grace. Too often their unworthiness is because of opposition to him. The sick minister even ties in his people's opposition to him and his policies to opposition to God!

The result of this weight-of-authority manipulation is that the minister uses "the cloth" to cover his nakedness. William E. Hulme says:

Since his identity as a person as well as a minister is tied up with the particular tangible credential, he espouses it with such authoritarian rigidity that he discourages any questioning either from within himself or from his people. The *show* must go on— this holy masquerade, as Olive Hartmann calls it. The laymen's expectations that demand too much of the minister constrain the insecure minister to demand too little of the layman. They

69

need simply believe what he tells them. He leads them into the same fraudulent security into which the pressure to justify his authority has driven him.[1]

The degree of his training. Another technique of the manipulator is reference to his training. Though he would never admit it, he "plays omniscient." He fires his college degrees and seminary training back at anyone who dares take potshots at his authority. *Impressing* rather than *expressing* characterizes his efforts.

Seldom does he fail to inform people of the number of years spent in preparation for his task. He drops the names of his professors here and there as he preaches or leads discussion groups. Instead of talking *with* people he talks *down to* them. If people do not respond to his preaching, he takes refuge in academics. "The reason must be that they are not able to grasp the depth of my thought." Insensitive to the feelings of people, he uses the congregation as an audience to receive his "word for the day." How privileged they are to have Dr. ———— as their minister!

This kind of manipulator practices "milk-bottle" preaching. The congregation is like a collection of empty milk bottles. His task is to flip open the caps of the bottles, pour in the milk that he has for the day, and send them on their way. Completely monological—no thought of dialogue, no concern with hearing needs!

The power of his privilege. All ministers know things about individuals and families that others do not know. In his position he has access to classified information.

[1] William E. Hulme, *Your Pastor's Problems: A Guide for Ministers and Laymen* (Garden City, N. Y.: Doubleday & Co., 1966), pp. 100-101.

The kind of information readily available to the minister tempts the minister to manipulate. The opportunity is great for the manipulator to use the information by playing on the person's guilt or by cleverly demanding that he act or participate in ways pleasing to the minister.

In a counseling situation a minister may receive information from one person which involves a number of others. Though this is confidential information, the manipulator (not by betraying a trust—he would never do this!) uses it to influence and control participation and cooperation.

The stacking of the deck. "Control" is the key word for the manipulator. The manipulative minister can never trust the democratic process. He feels a need to stack the deck, to control all the groups and committees in the church.

A manipulator does not believe that truth in the congregation should be arrived at by a process of checks and balances. He dominates by putting weak-egoed persons into places of leadership rather than risk choosing strong personalities. This can take on glaring proportions that are obvious to the outsider, but are often unrecognized by the manipulator. His manipulating has become a part of his nature. He has rationalized himself into thinking that all he does is for "the good of the church."

The manipulative minister will never let himself get in the position of being outvoted. An illustration of this came from a large congregation in desperate need of moving from the downtown heart of the city. More space was needed for building and parking. The building was run-down and in obvious need of repair. To repair and get it into halfway serviceable condition would require a substantial sum of money. It was the feeling of the denominational leaders, the minister, and a large number of the congregation officials that the move was necessary and inevitable. An official conference was set for a decision. Two days before the meeting the minister, because of direct verbal opposition from a few people whom he thought represented a larger number, began to feel that the vote would not favor a move. Finding no legitimate or technical reason for calling off the meeting, he faked an illness and persuaded the denominational leader to postpone the conference for another month. The issue would have passed, but the manipulator was not secure enough in his position to risk a vote.

Much of the time of the manipulator in clerics is spent in stacking the deck, rounding up the necessary votes, and organizing the congregation around those over whom he has complete control. He is most comfortable in a church made up of "little old ladies of both sexes."

Augustine warned that the very essence of idolatry is that we use what we ought to worship and worship what we ought to use. The deck-stacking manipulator practices idolatry in his use of persons. He sees them as pawns that he is to move about on the board of the church program, accomplishing his ends by directing all the activity, all the ideas, all the decisions, *all the time*. The relationship between him and other persons is necessarily an "I-it" and not an "I-thou" one. People are reduced to things.

The scarcity of his kind. An effective lever in the manipulative minister's effort at power and control is "the scarcity of his kind." Everyone now knows that there is a shortage of ministers—especially ministers!

In The United Methodist Church alone over twelve hundred new ministers are needed each year to fill the vacancies created by deaths and retirements. This is not to mention the countless expanding areas of ministry in which the church is constantly seeking to involve herself. With these valid facts in mind the sharp manipulator has one good way of getting his way. He lets the people know that they are short on alternatives.

All so casually a word is dropped about the pulpit committee that was in town last week talking to him. Or the less subtle, "Did you notice that group of people in church last Sunday? They were from St. John's Church. *You know their minister just resigned.*" The congregation is made aware of the opportunities that are knocking at his door. Thus they are stimulated to less opposition and more benefits for their "much-sought-after minister."

Moving Toward Actualization

In the last three chapters we will suggest specific ways in which individuals and congregations may throw off the shackles of manipulation and participate together in actualizing relationships. Here we want to indicate some principles that will start us on the road. Underscore again the fact that nowhere are we suggesting that a person or a congregation can become actualized in the fullest sense of the word. Nor do we wish to create a deep sense of guilt on the part of those who sense their manipulative systems. We do want to suggest the alternative of actualization as a style of life which will enable us to function more fully as persons and be the individuals we were created to be.

The priority of persons. Erich Fromm has said that things can be dissected or manipulated without damage to their nature, but man is not a thing. He cannot be dissected without being destroyed. He cannot be manipulated without being harmed. When the truth of this really burns into the life of the church—ministers and laymen alike—a major step will have been taken in the move from manipulation to actualization. *Persons have priority over programs.* When this is not the case, the ministry of the church is reduced to the level of the marketplace.

The church, then, must become the place where the primary characteristics of actualization can be expressed, accepted, appreciated, and cultivated. A person must be able to express himself and his feelings *honestly.* In the Christian community a person should, in fact, be able to *be* his feelings in a genuine fashion without fear of condemnation. The morning after a layman had expressed himself honestly in a meeting, he confronted his minister with the question, "Have I been excommunicated?" His assumption was that because he had expressed himself, he had disrupted the program. Consciously or unconsciously his experience in the church had taught him that programs are more important than persons. The actualizing response of the minister was: "The expression of your real feelings was a courageous thing. Thank you for being yourself. I appreciate it." Persons must have precedence over programs.

Appreciation of differences. Too often in the church efforts are made to squeeze persons into a mold, and any expression of differences is scorned, or at least frowned upon. Here dogma takes precedence over persons. The imposition of theological straitjackets is anathema in the actualizing church.

The distinctive mark of man is his *freedom.* This is one of the things that makes him like God. To retain that freedom

74

and to see that it is retained by others, to use it responsibly and to allow others the same opportunity, is necessary for the actualizing person and congregation. Rather than smothering the expression of the "I" on the part of any person, the Christian community should enhance the *awareness* of each individual "I" and provide the atmosphere of freedom and trust for the expression of it.

In the church the individual's capacity of awareness should be enhanced, especially at the interpersonal and ultrapersonal levels. Here the person should be stimulated to grow and share. This can be so only in an atmosphere of freedom and trust. Until the church can provide this setting, it will be a depressing rather than an exciting fellowship.

Ministry-laity relationships. One of the primary causes for manipulation in the church is false role expectation—where professionalism takes precedence over persons.

While the minister is a professional, he must never allow himself or his laymen to believe that he is a super Christian. He is an equal among equals. While his professional role puts him in a position of leadership and even in a position of power out of proportion to the power of others, it does not convey to him special value or worth. His professional status should never make for a top-dog–under-dog relationship. The actualizing minister continually resists the pressures to be made a top-dog, and must always resist the subtle economic pressures that would sometimes make him an under-dog.

Samuel W. Blizzard says that the *believer-saint* is traditionally a normative role for the minister. "The believer-saint is an exemplar for others to follow because he is dependent upon God. He conceives himself primarily as a 'man of faith' who humbly seeks God's will." [2] Not only does the minister some-times conceive himself in this fashion, it is not uncommon for the layman to demand that he play this role. The actualiz-ing minister and layman steadfastly resist this dichotomy. The minister is seen as a "player-coach." But he is still a player! A shared ministry is the aim of the actualizing church. Therefore, the minister is a struggler among strugglers, a be-liever among believers, a seeker among seekers, a servant among servants, and a sinner among sinners.

The *passive participant* is often the professional role ex-pectation of the layman. Yet in the actualizing relationship the ancient concept of the *laos,* the whole people of God, the priesthood of all believers, is sought. Ministers and laymen worship together, work together, study together, serve to-gether, and grow together.

The actualizing relationship of minister and layman is char-acterized by shared risk-taking. Both dare to resist the false role expectations and be themselves in honesty and openness. This is the heart of the actualizing relationship. Such daring involves the constant possibility of failure and disappointment, but also promises fulfillment that comes from real communion and that results from shared accomplishments.

[2] Wayne E. Oates, ed., *The Minister's Own Mental Health* (Man-hasset, N.Y.: Channel Press, 1961), p. 147.

Chapter IV
Manipulation vs. Actualization

Man, the Manipulator

Man in the process of growing up often seems to develop almost naturally a manipulative style. We have needs to influence others, and in doing so we develop tendencies to dominate and control. Rather than meeting and responding to others we try to manipulate and influence. We plan strategies in order to get the other person to do the thing we want. Life becomes a process of winning or losing. We plan tonight how to dominate and have our way tomorrow—whether it be a mother dominating a child, a businessman subjugating another, a man seducing a woman, a neighbor using a neighbor. *Our whole approach becomes one of trying to use friends and influence people.* This is the sickness of manipulation.

A manipulator we define as "a person who exploits, uses, or controls himself and others as 'things' in self-defeating ways." [1] We have defined some fundamental types of manipulators which are illustrated in Figure 1.

[1] This definition, Figure 1, and the material describing manipulative and actualizing types are taken from *Man, the Manipulator.* For a more comprehensive presentation of this material, the reader may refer to this volume.

Figure 1

THE MANIPULATIVE TYPES[2]

[2] The internal dimensions of this figure are adapted from Timothy Leary, *The Interpersonal Theory of Personality* (New York: The Ronald Press Company, 1957).

This is a picture of a typical therapy or Christian actualization group and, at the same time, a picture of each of us with our self-defeating manipulative techniques. The manipulator overexaggerates any one or a combination of these types. Usually when we are most strongly one type, we project its opposite onto others around us, making them our targets. A *weakling* wife, for instance, often chooses a husband who is a *dictator* and then controls him by her subversive devices.

So each of us, paradoxically, is such a group—a composite with all these manipulative potentials. Any therapeutic group is each of us turned inside out! This is why we shall see later that group relationships are so effective in helping the manipulator to see himself in others. The reason why we seem different to different people is that we expose only certain manipulations to some and other manipulations to others. Also this is why we must be careful not to judge another by other people's opinions. They have seen only certain aspects of the person.

The Actualizor

The alternative to the manipulator is the actualizor. The actualizor is defined as a person who appreciates himself and others as "thous" and who is turning his self-defeating manipulations into self-fulfilling potentials. While the manipulator is a many-faceted person of self-defeating opposites, the actualizor is a person of self-fulfilling opposites. The paradox is that the manipulator develops from the seed of the actualizor, and out of manipulative potentials can grow actualizing potentials. Figure 2 is a picture of the actualizing types and again a picture of the actualizing person as a combination of complementary potentials.[3]

[3] From *Man, the Manipulator.*

1. **From the dictator develops the leader.** The leader leads rather than dictates. He is forceful, yet not dominating. An example of an actualizing leader in history is Winston Churchill. Through World War II this great man exemplified leadership of the greatest democratic type.

The complementary opposite of the leader is the empathizer. The empathizer not only talks, but listens, and is aware of his weaknesses. He demands good work, yet accepts the human tendency to err. Such a person was Eleanor Roosevelt. She knew her personal limitations and empathized with the underdeveloped nations and peoples of the world in her work with the United Nations.

The actualizor integrates both his leadership and empathy. A person who demonstrated such integration was Adlai Stevenson, who had the ability to stand firm in the United Nations and at the same time tune in sensitively to all the voices of the world.

2. **From the calculator develops the respecter.** Rather than using or exploiting, the actualizor respects himself and others as "thous" rather than "things." Such a person was Mahatma Gandhi. This man in his nonviolence always deeply respected those with whom he dealt.

The complementary opposite of the respecter is the appreciator. The appreciator does not simply depend on others, but appreciates the different skills that others have to offer. He appreciates points of view different from his own and does not need to have other people think as he thinks. Pope John XXIII illustrated the appreciator in his ambassadorship with other world religions.

The actualizor integrates both his respect and appreciation. Such an integration we see in the great Jewish theologian,

Figure 2

THE ACTUALIZING TYPES

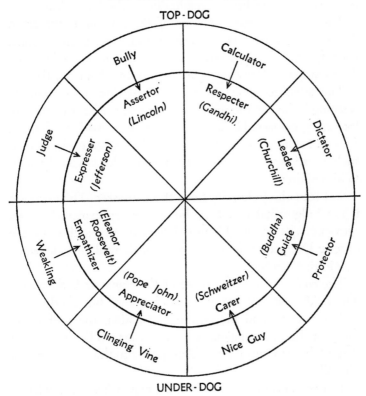

Martin Buber. To him, each person was unique, irreplaceable, particular, and not the repetition of any other—he was a "thou."

3. **From the bully develops the assertor.** The assertor enjoys a worthy foe, but he is direct and straightforward. He is

81

not hostile and dominating as is the bully. Abraham Lincoln showed this characteristic in the famous Lincoln-Douglas debates as well as in his leadership during the Civil War.

The complementary opposite of the assertor is the carer. The carer is not the obsequious nice guy, yet is affectionate, friendly, and deeply loving. Albert Schweitzer, in his deep devotion to the African people, showed this characteristic.

The actualizor integrates both his assertion and caring. He is strong in his interpersonal relations and yet has the capacity for caring contact. He integrates aggression with tenderness. John F. Kennedy, in his handling of the Cuban crisis, showed such assertion, and yet one is reminded of his tender devotion to his children.

4. **From the judge develops the expresser.** The expresser is not judgmental of others, but is able to express his own convictions strongly. Thomas Jefferson, the author of the historic Declaration of Independence, showed this characteristic in that writing.

The complementary opposite of the expresser is the guide. The guide does not protect or teach others, but gently helps each person to find his own way. Buddha, the founder of the great Eastern religion, was such a man. His dictum was that each man must find "the way" up the mountain for himself.

The actualizor integrates both his expression and guidance. The actualizor does not think *for* others, but *with* them. He helps others to help themselves by his own expression of views and yet gives each the right to make his own decisions. The Sermon on the Mount was deeply expressive, and yet the Beatitudes were *invitations,* not demands. Such was the actualizing nature of Jesus.

82

As may be seen, the truly actualizing person is one who has achieved integration of the opposite sides of his nature. He is like the ice skater who freely skates from one potential to another, employing each creatively in his movement through life.

The conditions that create the change from manipulation to actualization are still somewhat of a mystery. The changes of Saul the dictator to Paul the leader and Simon the bully to Peter the assertor illustrate the fact that such change is possible. In our experience the Christian actualization group, which we will discuss in Chapter VII, provides the conditions for change and stimulates the total church to be transformation-centered.

Two Approaches to Living

The more we consider the patterns of manipulation and actualization, the more certain we are that there are two basic approaches to living. One has to do with *being*, the other with *doing, acting, proving, and trying*. The following chart shows these two stances in contrast.

MANIPULATION	ACTUALIZATION
Doing—Going through the motions	Being—Core living: genuine, wholehearted, expressing one's selfhood
Acting—Artificial behavior	
Proving—The idealized image	
Trying—Effort vs. surrender	
1. Defending or regretting the past, fearing, promising, or predicting the future.	1. Trusting the present moment, being oneself as fully as possible.

2. "Should-ism" or "about-ism." Preserving and enhancing the self of the past or the future.

3. Teaching others in an effort to convince onself.

4. *Im*pressing: manipulating.

5. Altruism, fairness, obligation—using a system.

6. Faith in figuring: "What can I do?" "Will it do any good?"

7. Believing in tricks, controlling, manipulating.

8. Basic responsibility seen as living for others. "Helping."

9. Avoiding risk: insuring, avoiding hurt, pleasing.

10. Respect for others first. "Don't be selfish."

11. Resorting to analysis of others to avoid introspection.

12. Trying to control others. "What can I do to keep him?" (child, spouse).

2. Living: "*is*-ism." Accepting life as it *is* in the here and now. Accepting oneself "as I am."

3. Learning by experiencing the moment.

4. *Ex*pressing: being.

5. Freedom: being, giving and receiving freely.

6. Faith in feeling and trusting: expression of one's feelings.

7. Believing in self-expression as a basis for relating to others.

8. Basic responsibility seen as awareness of one's own needs; loyalty to oneself.

9. Risking relationships by honest expression of feelings.

10. Respect for self first.

11. Openness to self-evaluation or change.

12. Allowing others to be themselves with the right to do as they wish.

84

13. Believing life can be what one prefers or demands it to be, what we feel we are entitled to have it be.

13. Accepting life with its joys and sorrows.

14. "Exhibiting" strength only.

14. Being courageous (accepting strengths and weaknesses).

15. Motive for action: What will others think?

15. Motive for action: What is my feeling at the moment?

16. Trying to change others.

16. Communicating with others.

17. Expression of "good" feelings and repression of "bad" feelings.

17. Awareness and expression of one's feelings.

18. Trying to avoid the "consequences" of being oneself.

18. Trusting one's ability to handle the "consequences" of being oneself.

19. Driven by a need to maintain the appearance of perfection.

19. Driven by a need for ever increasing improvement, but recognizing perfection as not fully attainable as a human being.

20. Doing what is expected by others and expecting others to do what you expect of them.

20. Doing only what is deeply felt within one's being.

21. Measuring up to external

21. Living in terms of inner

expectations: standards, *duties*, obligations or rules.

fulfillment of wants, likes, dislikes, values.

22. Moral values are aped in a counterfeit, phony way but are all the while secretly felt to be a burdensome imposition.

22. Moral values are evaluated and assimilated rather than swallowed and then resented. Values are then accepted as an expression of self-discipline.

23. Fear of making mistakes, recognizing any shortcomings, or anticipating any failure.

23. Mistakes are accepted as natural and human.

24. Criticism is seen as an intolerable threat to self-esteem.

24. Criticism is welcomed and is evaluated as an opportunity for growth.

25. Fear of pursuing wishes of one's own unless justified as necessary to health, altruism, education, or other "socially proclaimed" values.

25. Pursuit of self-interest is seen as "divine self-expression" and not opposed to interest in others.

26. Equating knowledge about a virtue with possessing that virtue.

26. Being is seen as a process of attaining, never as attainment.

27. Demanding approval from others as the criterion for being "right."

27. Utilizing self-approval as the ultimate criterion for behavior.

28. Seeing life as trying, effort to justify one's existence by planned productivity.

28. Seeing life can be lived as a relaxed expression of one's being, with its limitations.

29. Worshiping God as he is imagined to be, "without" or "up there."

29. Following God as he is expressed from within one's being.

Three Levels of Awareness

A central thesis of this volume is that the experience of man exists at three levels of awareness:

    I. Self and Self
   II. Self and Others
  III. Self and God

We call these the intrapersonal, the interpersonal, and the ultrapersonal levels of awareness. As you will see from the following discussion, these three levels must not be narrowly construed, especially the third level. This thesis stems from the great commandment: "You shall love the Lord your God with all your heart, and with all your soul, and with all your mind. This is the great and first commandment. And a second is like it, You shall love your neighbor as yourself. On these two commandments depend all the law and the prophets" (Matt. 22:37-40). We assume that this trinity is especially integrated in the actualizing person. A person cannot be actualizing if one of these elements is missing.

I. SELF AND SELF

In our society perhaps one of the most common misconceptions of loving is that it is sinful to love oneself. Erich Fromm has done much to help us understand this misconception. He says, "Love of others and love of ourselves are not alternatives. On the contrary, an attitude of love towards themselves will be found in all those who are capable of loving others." [4] Here Fromm suggests that love of another and love of oneself are essentially integrated. Sullivan has said it another way, "As you love yourself, so shall you love others. Strange, but true, but with no exceptions."

To be fully aware of ourselves is an idea that many are not at all acquainted with. Most of us are strangers to ourselves and need a get-acquainted opportunity. We go through life without any contact with our real self. In a popular way this malady is seen in the thousands who sit in baseball stadiums with their transistor radios clutched to their ears. They are in tune with the game they are viewing. Consider how curious is the phenomenon. They are seeing the game firsthand, but they do not trust their own experiencing. So, watching the game, they listen to the announcer who is the "professional experiencer." Their assumption is: he sees it better, he says it better, he feels it better. What is happening is obvious. The "radio clutchers" are dependent upon the announcer's telling them what he sees and feels so that they may properly see and feel, for they do not trust their own perceptions and feelings.

It may be that the hippie movement with its obsession for awareness is a rebellion against our progressive inability to feel and to express our feelings. It is surprising how few people have even a slight understanding of what they feel or allow themselves to become even faintly aware of their own

[4] *The Art of Loving* (New York: Harper & Row, 1956), p. 59.

feelings. In one of his prayers Malcolm Boyd reveals the struggle of a person who is wrestling through a get-acquainted session with his own feelings.

I wasn't going to get lonely any more, and so I kept very busy, telling myself I was serving you. But it's getting dark again, and I'm alone; honestly, Lord, I'm lonely as hell.

Why do I feel so sorry for myself? There's no reason why I should be. You're with me, and I know it. I'll be with other people in a little while. I know some of them love me very much in their own way, and I love some of them very much in mine.

But I still feel so damned lonely right now, in this minute that I'm living. I feel confused about how to get through the immediate next few steps to the other ones afterward. It's silly, but I feel this way because I'm threatened by me, and I wish I could get through me to you, clearly and with a kind of purity and integrity.

And yet, while I say this to you, I've been unkind to certain people whom you also love, and I've added to misunderstanding and confusion, and I haven't been able to make it at all nicely or properly.

Take hold of me, and connect me with these other lives, Jesus. Give me patience and love so that I can listen when I plug into these other lives. Help me to listen and listen and listen . . . and love by being quiet and serving, and being there.[5]

This is an expression of deep feeling. It destroys the conventional distance between prayer and the ordinary life. One can feel in reading the words that though the depth of loneliness is experienced and expressed, here is one who is in com-

---

[5] From *Are You Running with Me, Jesus?* by Malcolm Boyd. Copyright © 1965 by Malcolm Boyd. Reprinted by permission of Holt, Rinehart and Winston, Inc.

munion with himself and thus is capable of communion with others and with God.

II. SELF AND OTHERS

The second level of awareness is the relationship of self and others. Perhaps the most fundamental relationship in life is that of relating to others. Human at-onement is a necessary dimension of living. But the paradox is that we know so very little about what it means to really love one another. Real love of another involves three fundamental dimensions:

1. In order to love others we must *appreciate them as "thous" and cease treating them as "things."* People are not products which we are committed to change, but persons with whom we cooperate for mutual growth. (For the reader who wishes to understand this idea better, this is the theme of *Man, the Manipulator*.)

2. To truly love another we must *commit* ourselves to that relationship. Another way of saying it is that we must *choose* to love another, and still another way to say it is that love is a decision, a judgment, or a choice. The average man says he "fell in love"—it happened to him. In contrast, the actualizor chooses to love. Love, then, is a decision to commit one's life to another. As Erich Fromm says, "This is, indeed, the rationale behind the idea of the unsolubility of marriage. . . . To love someone is more than just a strong feeling—it is a decision."

3. To love another means *taking the risk of asking the other to love you.* To choose to love another means to give complete trust to another, and this is very difficult. Most of us run, pretend not to see or be seen, try to be objective or rational—anything except unconditionally choosing to love another.

There are several ways in which we manipulatively avoid the choice. First we pretend to love everybody, and by a generalized loving of everybody, we avoid the reality of a deep grasp of an I-thou relationship. We substitute charm and friendliness for responsible and intimate loving. We substitute the glad-hand of making friends and influencing people for the intensity of a caring relationship. "This choice to love is an affirmation of the reality of God between myself and another, and though the other refuses to be affirmed, I have chosen to love and to affirm God and can, with deepened grief, not lose that hallowed light. In a true choice to love we ask for love in return; but we do not examine and demand and set quantities and qualities of ourself. Have I the courage to choose to love, to affirm another life, to offer another the best gift of my heart, and let him be what he is?" [6]

An even more difficult task is that of asking the one we have chosen to love us. To ask another to love us is a profoundly humble task. And again, many of us manipulatively hide from such conscious and open asking. We hedge; we give symbols of our love—a mink coat, a dozen roses—we ask proof; we say, "Prove that you love me." This is a way of avoiding the courage to respond. We ask another to admire some mask of ourselves. We act charming, flirtatious; we hide, lie, or deceive because we are afraid to ask another to really love our frail and mortal selves. To really love another, therefore, is to have made contact with him, to have penetrated his core with our core, instead of dealing with him at a level of tricks and manipulations.

[6] Robert Raynolds, *The Choice to Love* (New York: Harper & Row, 1959), p. 137.

III. SELF AND GOD

The third level of experience is that of self and God. We may at times forget who we are, but it is well-nigh impossible to forever *deny* what we are—namely, one made in the image and likeness of God. Pascal said, "We are something and we are not everything." We are creatures who are the bearers of an infinite capacity and an infinite intention.

The reason that manipulation is such a self-defeating style of life lies precisely in this fact: because we are who we are, we can never happily become the pawns of manipulative forces. This sense of identity, often hidden or deliberately repressed, is the source of any wholeness that we may know. It is certainly the ultimate call to an actualizing life.

The marvelous accomplishments of psychotherapy, psychology, and other adventures in self-discovery bring us to the threshold of real self-actualization as we become aware of this third level of experience. Deep calls unto deep, and we know that we were not intended for fear but for freedom, not for slavery but for sonship. Our real humanity is rooted in our relationship to God, and our boldest step in actualization is in responding to the ultimate claims of life.

Viktor Frankl underscored this when he wrote of his prison experience, "Psychological observations of the prisoners have shown that only the men who allowed their inner hold on their moral and spiritual selves to subside eventually fell victim to the camp's degenerating influences." [7] Man simply does not live by bread alone. While there may be evidence that different all-pervasive drives such as pleasure, sex, autonomy, etc., give man meaning, this meaning is not complete apart from

[7] *Man's Search for Meaning*, p. 110.

an awareness of his true identity—an identity that is known in relation to the ultrapersonal level of life.

While science does not give us an empirical concept of God, poets and philosophers have expressed this ultrapersonal level in a way which we cannot deny. Maslow's concept of the "peak experience" as the most wonderful experience of life provides a point at which science and philosophy meet to symbolize the experience of God. With perfect artistry Browning traced the moments of such experiences:

> Just when we are safest, there's a sunset-touch,
> A fancy from a flower-bell, some one's death,
> A chorus-ending from Euripides,—
> And that's enough for fifty hopes and fears
> As old and new at once as nature's self,
> To rap and knock and enter in our soul,
> Take hands and dance there, a fantastic ring,
> Round the ancient idol, on his base again,—
> The grand Perhaps! [8]

Job affirmed the genuine meeting when he exclaimed,

> I had heard of thee by the hearing of the ear,
> but now my eye sees thee.

God is really no stranger to the heart. We may define him differently and use different terminology to express his being, yet this in itself verifies the reality of this level of our experience. The other levels of awareness—self to self and self to others—are confirmed at their most authentic level by this ultrapersonal awareness.

[8] From "Bishop Blougram's Apology."

When Martin Buber wanted to put the crowning touch on his classic work, *I and Thou,* he did it by talking about the eternal *Thou.* Not only so, he did it by speaking of God in terms of *what he is in his relation to man.* And he talked in terms of "Person."

As a Person God gives personal life, he makes us as persons become capable of meeting with him and with one another. But no limitation can come upon him as the absolute Person, either from us or from our relations with one another; in fact we can dedicate to him not merely our persons but also our relations to one another. The man who turns to him therefore need not turn away from any other *I-Thou* relation; but he properly brings them to him, and lets them be fulfilled "in the face of God." [9]

The experience of God on such a level is inseparably linked with living. It is not primarily a *thought* experience, that is, a *belief* that God exists—as we have often made it in the church. Rather it is an experience. For some, perhaps for most, the experience will be the expression of living principles such as we normally associate with absolute Person: love, justice, truth, mercy, and forgiveness. So the actualizing person is content to be his expressions of God and to reflect those expressions in his action and relationships. He does not need to continually give sermons about it. The heart of actualization at this third level is not some opinion about God such as philosophy may reach in conclusion to its arguments; it is a personal relationship and a personal expression.

[9] (2nd ed.; New York: Charles Scribner's Sons, 1958), p. 136.

MANIPULATION VS. ACTUALIZATION

Figure 3

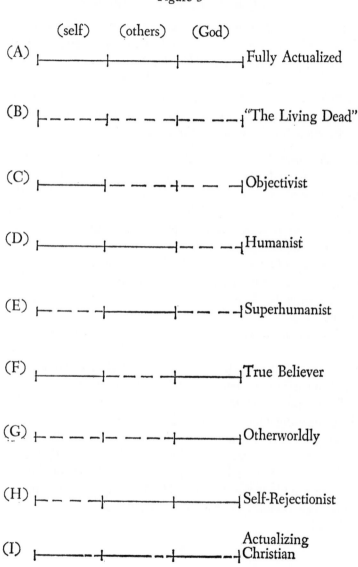

Living at All Levels of Awareness

Life at its fullest, in the actualizing sense, is lived at these three levels of awareness. Any effort to isolate one level of awareness from another is self-defeating.

Figure 3 compares some styles of life that fail to integrate these levels of awareness. It should be noted that our designation of these styles is not necessarily equivalent to the similar designations in the mind of the reader.

Line **A** shows the pattern of the *fully actualized* person. The continuous, unbroken line indicates an experiencing on the intrapersonal, the interpersonal, and the ultrapersonal levels.

B is a picture of *"the living dead."* In a sense, the most seriously deteriorated schizophrenic who is unaware of any level of contact is an example of this.

C is the *objectivist,* the self-glorifier. He limits his level of awareness to the intrapersonal. Nothing is real or of value outside himself. This is self-centeredness carried to its extreme.

D is the *humanist,* who experiences awareness on the intrapersonal and the interpersonal levels. He takes no time or makes no effort to seek or explore any level of awareness beyond himself or the person to whom he is relating.

E is what we call the *superhumanist.* He is the person who finds meaning only in others. He fails to develop his own inner potentials or explore any ultrapersonal level. Busy serving others, he never serves himself. Often his serving is limited to surface relationships and the giving of himelf to causes and demonstrations. He is incapable of core relationships because he has never become aware of his own selfhood.

F is the *true believer,* the one who is interested only in self and God. Salvation for him is intensely personal and usually means salvation from punishment in some future life by giving himself to God in this life. In this pattern there is an emphasis on self-awareness, though this is often negative. There is no feeling for others, or any compunction about interpersonal relationships.

G is the *otherworldly person* who might be called a "cloud-land liver." His thoughts are only of the ultrapersonal level of awareness. Self is denounced; "worldly" activity is scorned, and all effort is focused on the "other world."

H is the *self-rejectionist,* who renounces self in the service of God and others. Self-consideration is cast off, and utter dependence upon God is central. Service to others is the choice of involvement. The Puritans, as well as many priests and ministers, are sterling examples of this.

I is the *actualizing Christian.* He experiences awareness at all three levels though never perfectly, as the broken line in each level of awareness indicates. He is aware of his human potential and limitation, his relatedness to others, and is constantly seeking awareness for meaning at the third level.

While this brief presentation does not do justice to the sickness of man that causes him to function short of full awareness on these three levels, it is hoped that what we have said here will stimulate the reader to examine his own life-style in light of these three levels.

Chapter V
The Christian Actualizing Style of Life

In Chapter I we discussed the general characteristics of all actualizing as *honesty, awareness, freedom* and *trust.* We now propose that there is a specifically Christian actualizing style of life. Jesus is the indicator of the primary way. His life is the unique witness to the fact that we do not have to live as manipulators. He shatters the chains of enslavement, setting us free to become the persons God intended us to be.

Jesus was the one person in history who brought together the theory and practice of religion. "It was said to the men of old, 'You shall not. . . . But I say to you. . . .'" Through the words he spoke, the people he encountered, and the decisive actions he took, Jesus' life fulfilled a specific style of actualization. Maslow defined the characteristics of a self-actualizing person as a composite of all the subjects he had studied. No one person possessed them all. Jesus, on the other hand, not only proposed the characteristics of the Christian actualizor, but brought them together in a unique style of life. The Beatitudes are a significant expression of the Christian actualizing style which he incarnated.

The Actualizing Rhythm of Man

Figure 4 is a presentation of the Beatitudes in terms of the rhythm of the actualizing polarities of man. The essence of the Christian actualizing style lies in the capacity to experience the different dimensions, or polarities, of our existence as Jesus expressed them in the Beatitudes and witnessed to them in his own life. He intended these behavior principles to be understood as synergistic—not as an either/or, but as a rhythmic oscillating mode which is essential to the real nature of man.

In the following analysis each Beatitude is shown to have both an active and a passive dimension. This is the creative nature of Christ's teaching; he does not recommend a lock-step control of life, but a free spontaneous range of rhythmic expression in which we may find our freedom to be.

The deep wisdom expressed in the Beatitudes is the recognition of this implicit rhythm of life. Just as the human heart must function by active and passive movement, just as day is active and night passive, spring active and winter passive, so man, God's finest creation, must have his natural rhythm to be fully expressive of his potential.

The following discussion, an extension of the basic theory of *Man, the Manipulator,* is an attempt to describe the implicit rhythmic pattern of man's basic nature.

I.   The actualizor expresses himself rhythmically on the continuum of *strength* and *weakness.*

    A.   In the first Beatitude, Jesus says that the "blessed," or the joyous actualizor is *"poor in spirit."* To be poor in spirit means the opposite of having pride. Man is human, not God, with all the strengths of man

99

Figure 4

THE ACTUALIZING RHYTHM AS EXPRESSED IN THE BEATITUDES [1]

Active Dimension		Passive Dimension
I. Strength-Weakness Continuum	Poor in Spirit (Humanness)	
A. Expresses Strength	Mourn	Expresses Weakness
B. Develops Capacity to Handle Hurt	(Courage to Hurt)	Expresses Hurt
II. Control-Dependency Continuum	Meekness (Open to Limitations)	
A. Expresses Self-sufficiency	Hungers After Righteousness	Expresses Dependency
B. Awareness of Fulfillment	(Ethical Awareness)	Expresses Wants and Needs
III. Judging-Guidance Continuum	Merciful (Compassion)	
A. Expresses Negative Feelings	Persecuted	Forgives Injuries
B. Creatively Indifferent to Persecution	(Acceptance of)	Learns from Enemies
IV. Aggression-Caring Continuum	Peacemaker (Assertive Caring)	
A. Asserts Convictions	Pure in Heart	Loves Enemies
B. Aware of Potential	(Honesty-Integration)	Accepts Imperfection

[1] Although there are nine Beatitudes, it should be noted that the ninth is an extension of the eighth. Further, the scriptural sequence has been changed in the above chart. See Matt. 5:3-12.

and all the weaknesses as well. He is aware of his strength ("a little less than the angels"), and yet he must also be aware of his weaknesses. As the Son of man, Jesus was tempted and felt his humanness in the wilderness, and yet in the temple, as he rebuked the moneychangers, he was aware of his strength.

B. In the second Beatitude, Jesus says, "Blessed are those who *mourn*." Here it is clear that to mourn means to feel hurt, to experience suffering. To experience hurt means that we must be aware again of our human weakness—aware that we can be "gotten to." It also means to trust our capacity to experience hurt; it therefore leads to an increasing belief in our capacity to take misfortune or suffering, and therefore paradoxically helps us experience our strength. On the other hand, the courage to mourn with others empathetically provides them courage as they discover their strength. Through the pain he experienced as he wrestled with his destiny, even to the point of sweating blood, Jesus found the courage to face his own crucifixion.

II. The actualizor expresses himself rhythmically on the continuum of *dependency* and *self-control*.

A. In the third Beatitude, Jesus described the actualizing life as one characterized by *meekness*. To be meek is to be open to our limitations. It means expressing our dependency when it is felt and yet at the same time being aware of our self-sufficiency and independence. Jesus said, "He who has seen me has seen the Father." He spoke as one having

101

authority. Yet at the same time he did not judge. He did not even need to "play God" and forgive. He merely said, "Go, and do not sin again."

B. In the fourth Beatitude, Jesus characterized the actualizor as *hungering after righteousness*. To hunger after righteousness means ethical awareness. It means asking for what we need or want, but being aware of what we do not need for fulfillment. As with Maslow's actualizors, the Christian actualizor knows what is right and wrong and seeks what is right for him. Jesus expressed his hunger after righteousness even at an early age as he visited the temple and talked with the priests. He also knew what he did not need—the power and security which was promised him by the Tempter in the wilderness.

III. The actualizor expresses himself rhythmically on the continuum of *judging* and *guidance*.

A. In the fifth Beatitude, Jesus talks of the importance of being *merciful*. To be merciful means to be understanding of others and to have compassion. It means being able to forgive injuries, but at the same time to express strong negative feelings regarding the behavior of those whom we love and disagreement with others without judging their rightness or wrongness. Expressing feelings still keeps the dialogue open, while making judgments closes it. Jesus was merciful when he said, "Let him who is without sin among you be the first to throw a stone." Yet he rebuked the Pharisees when he felt strongly negative toward their critical self-righteousness.

B. In the eighth Beatitude, Jesus said, "Blessed are those who are *persecuted*." Here, he implies that from misunderstanding and disapproval we can grow. We can learn from our enemies. We can develop a creative indifference to persecution. We can guide others without making their decisions for them. Jesus loved Judas even though Judas betrayed him, and by his affirmation on the cross Jesus was *creatively* indifferent to persecution—"Father, forgive them; for they know not what they do."

IV. The actualizor expresses himself rhythmically on the continuum of *aggression* and *caring*.

A. The seventh Beatitude describes the Christian actualizor as a *peacemaker*. To make peace means to make peace not only with others, but with ourselves, to assert our convictions yet be compassionate and caring. Jesus was a peacemaker; he would not let Peter fight his enemies, and yet he himself was willing to die for what he believed. He aggressively stated his convictions in the Sermon on the Mount, and yet he asked God to forgive those who crucified him.

B. The sixth Beatitude describes the Christian actualizor as *pure in heart*. In a real sense this Beatitude integrates all the others. As Kierkegaard has so succinctly stated, to be pure in heart is to will one thing. This suggests the ability to integrate one's awareness of potential along with the acceptance of one's limitations. In Maslow's terms the actualizing person is synergistic; he has resolved his dichotomies. Jesus was a centered person. Though he humanly prayed, "Let this cup pass," he subordinated that desire to God's will for his life. "Nevertheless, not as I will, but as thou wilt." He aggressively cared to fulfill his life's mission.

The Beatitudes not only describe the polarities of human existence, but *invite* us to participate in the process of actualization and blessedness through an increasing awareness of the natural polarities that God has created within us. We are seeking this as we call for a Christian actualizing style. But *how* is this accomplished? This is the question we must consider now.

Jesus as a Model

"It is only when a person exists according to the mode that is appropriate to him that he is responsible and capable of healthy activity; without this he is only the pale follower, a being who dogs the footsteps of others and is deprived of his own personality." This word of C. G. Jung must be remembered by those seeking the Christian actualizing style. We have our own *élan*, our own individual freedom of expression. Unlike the Hemingway, Bond, or *Playboy* life-styles, the Christian actualizing style does not call for image imitation which centers on superficial accouterments or conformity. There may be "manners" which can be acquired by the Christian or a code of conduct by which he can live, but this is not *the* manner nor is it *the* style. Though there are multitudes of witnesses to the Christian actualizing style—

Dietrich Bonhoeffer, Martin Luther King, Jr., Evelyn Under-hill, Florence Allshorn—we are not to seek to copy them. We do find in them vital attempts that speak to us. The unique image, however, is Jesus Christ, and our uniqueness is found in seeking identification with this model.

The uniqueness of Christian actualization in relation to other forms of actualization is that in Jesus, God reveals what it means to be a man, and through God's Spirit calls forth our own unique personal expression of Christian actualization potentials. Through him we are made aware of the many facets of our uniqueness and are called to fulfill them. Thus he makes it possible for each of us to be a man after his like-ness through developing the *unique* personality which is ours. This is what Paul is talking about when he speaks of being "conformed to the image of his Son [Christ]" (Rom. 8:29) or having Christ "formed in you" (Gal. 4:19). For the person who would seek the Christian actualizing style Jesus reveals the true nature of man and offers him the opportunity to share in the "sonship" of God. In this sense Jesus is "the Way."

The real uniqueness of the Christian style, therefore, lies not in a set of characteristics of actualization other than hon-esty, awareness, freedom, and trust but in the way these characteristics are combined and integrated in the life of Jesus to provide the model of the kind of men we are to be. What really matters in a Christian actualizing style is *being* —an inner faith, an inner conviction, an inner belief in one-self, and a commitment to the ultimate in life.

Life on earth is life in the making. Through the continuous making of resolute decisions man patterns his life and molds his character. This is what Erich Fromm was talking about when he wrote: "Decisions are not made on some final day but early in one's development. Life is a process of degrees in freedom. Most people fail not because they are bad, they fail because they do not wake up to see that sometime at a fork in the road they have to decide. They are not aware when life asks them a question and they still have an alternative answer." [2]

Basic to this life of choice for the actualizing Christian is his ultimate commitment to life as he finds it revealed in Jesus. From him we learn that to be a person requires *voluntary commitment*—a willingness to accept the responsibility for the development and expression of our unique potentials. It is through this commitment that our style takes form. We discover our potential; our relationships to self, others, and God are transformed, we create our own unique contribution. We make choices from day to day in light of the ultimate choice we have already made.

This commitment, then, defines our freedom. However, we are not "to freedom condemned," but rather "to freedom freed." God did not manipulate Jesus into the expression of his unique potentials. The choice was always his. The choice is always ours. Life does not just happen, nor does it remain absurd, as Sartre insists. Life is given by God, and our commitment to him not only gives meaning to our existence as we seek to actualize our potentials, but through this commitment our freedom is enhanced and disciplined.

Thus the Christian actualizing style goes beyond Maslow's theory of self-actualization. This style involves not only the realization and expression of our unique personal potentials,

[2] *The Heart of Man: Its Genius for Good and Evil*, Ruth N. Anshen, ed. (New York: Harper & Row, 1964).

but calls us to something beyond ourselves. A tension is kept between the "I am" and the "I ought." "If I believe in something," says Gabriel Marcel, "it means that I place myself at the disposal of something, or again that I pledge myself fundamentally, and this pledge affects not only *what I have* but also *what I am.*" So, while we have our own *élan*, Jesus is our *élan vital*, our Life Force.

The Symbol of the Style

Joe Saul, John Steinbeck's character in *Burning Bright*, was past middle age, and the one fear of his life was that he would die without offspring to bear his name. His first wife had been incapable of bearing children. Now married to another, he was again haunted by this fear. When his wife shared the news of the expected child, he became delirious with joy. He confided to a close friend: "I want to bring a present to her, . . . something like a ceremony, something like a golden sacrament, some pearl like a prayer or a red flaming ruby of thanks. That's compulsion on me. . . . I must get this thing. My joy requires a symbol." Joy does require a symbol. Men have always employed symbols and imagery to bring to the fore the meaning of life. The pattern of life suggested by the Christian actualizing style is also best communicated by symbol.

The *dance* is our symbol for the Christian actualizing style. We have seen that Jesus not only is our model of the actualizing style by making us aware of the many facets of our uniqueness, but that he inspirits us as we participate in the process of actualization. Through commitment to the possibility of new life as it is revealed in him we find freedom to be the persons we are destined to be. The dance best symbolizes the integral quality of the characteristics of actualization—honesty, awareness, freedom, and trust—with the unique expression of the Christian actualizing style. As Sister Mary Corita has been quoted as saying, "If we left it to the spirit, all we would have is Jesus and dancing."

The essential quality of the dance which makes it an expressive symbol for the Christian actualizing style is *spontaneous creative response*. To move in fixed patterns or stylized steps is to miss the meaning of the dance—to respond creatively to music and rhythm is to know the ultimate joy of dancing.

In the Christian actualizing style we do not seek to control life, rather we respond to it. One never knows the joys of dancing simply by observing others as they dance. A total personal involvement in rhythm, sound, and movement is required. So also with the Christian actualizing style. But how can we be honest? How can we trust another? How can we risk intimacy and self-disclosure? We prefer the hell of a predictable situation to the joy that may come from an unpredictable one. It is only when we respond to each other, involving ourselves in the dance, and seek to appropriate the style of the Christian actualizor that we develop the capacity to respond to each new situation in freedom and trust. Naturally this spontaneity grows and develops as we consciously practice the actualizing way. But even in the beginning we experience a freedom to *move* and *be* because we are not bound by the need to predict and control. This is what we call response-ability, the ability to respond with a liveness in the present moment to the aliveness of another. This is possible because of our awareness of who we are and what life is all about.

Thomas C. Oden reminds us that human existence is characterized by three fundamental questions: (1) How do I fail to actualize the self I envision as true and good? (2) What new options for self-understanding confront me through which I might perceive some new mode of self-fulfillment? (3) If such possibilities exist, how can they be actualized? The Christian actualizing person is *aware* of the conflicts in the polarities of his nature and also the inherent possibilities. He has heard and seen the word of possibility in Christ and therefore confronts these questions out of his relationship to Christ. It is this relationship that intensifies our awareness and enables us to respond to persons and situations spontaneously and creatively rather than to react controllingly.

This spontaneity and creativity is the essence of the dance. The Christian actualizor responds to life by giving himself to life the way the dancer gives himself to the dance. Jesus' life provides the model for creative and spontaneous relationships. The stern demands made of the rich young ruler were quite different from the understanding compassion shown the woman at the well.

By showing us our forgiveness and acceptance by God, Jesus enables us to cast off our false pretensions and illusions and frees us to be honest and spontaneous. He reminds us of the persons we really are and provides us the power to be those persons. Therefore, risk-taking involvement becomes our style.

This involvement has special meaning in interpersonal relationships. There are times when we dance alone, rare moments when we respond to the world around and within us, unaware of other people and other worlds. But as David A. Gibbons says, "Most of the basic rhythms of life are rhythms which call for partners, for fellow dancers whose responses to life evoke creativity in us, whose common willingness to risk the novel, to dare the new, supports us in our venture."

In the traditional social dance there is usually an active and a passive partner—a leader and a follower. Again this is an external expression of our active and passive polarities. As each partner involves himself in the dance, the polarities dissolve, and there is a natural atunement to each other so that the two partners perform as one. This is the symbol of actualizing integration.

Because the actualizing person is in touch with and can be honest about what he feels, thinks, is, and does, he manifests and gives of himself clearly, directly, specifically. He receives other persons' responses as gifts and as opportunities for learning and growing. He regards the communications of others with wonder, awe, and acceptance, not as expressions of an enemy or a competitor. As he grows in the free expression of the Christian actualizing style, he responds creatively.

In the Christian actualizing style we *contact* our partners, and we dance together. We have a deep feeling of identification with others. Jesus as our model is especially vivid here. The self-expression and self-giving of Jesus are his most unique characteristics. He initiated his ministry by this declaration of intent:

> The Spirit of the Lord is upon me,
> because he has anointed me to preach good news to the poor.
> He has sent me to proclaim release to the captives

and recovering of sight to the blind,
to set at liberty those who are oppressed.

The interpersonal dimension of our dance calls us to an expenditure of ourselves beyond the limits of calculation and rationality. When we know through Christ that we are loved by God, then we can love ourselves—and loving ourselves, we can then love others and identify ourselves with them, rejoicing with those who rejoice and weeping with those who weep.

Embracing the Style

John David Maguire reminds us that the fundamental gesture of the dance is the embrace. We cannot offer a "one-two-three" for developing the Christian actualizing style. We can simply say *embrace it!* In the next two chapters ways for the embrace within the church are offered, but in the final test the individual must take the risk of embracing it for himself.

Very early in his book *The Courage to Be* Paul Tillich sets the stage for his theme by saying that "the courage to be is the ethical act in which man affirms his own being in spite of these elements of his existence which conflict with his essential self-affirmation." [3] In the Christian actualizing style we become conscious of our true self, and despite circumstances our true self is not threatened. "Winning the game" is not essential for self-dignity and self-worth as it is in manipulative styles.

At the heart of this is the awareness that we *are* unique persons. This uniqueness is a gift of God. We accept it, cease

[3] (New Haven: Yale University Press, 1952), p. 3.

backing away from it, and busy ourselves *being our potential*. Fulfillment comes when we feel we are becoming what we have the possibility of becoming.

Imagine a duck who has been stranded on dry land in the midst of a drought. The sun beats down upon him, and he waddles about on the parched and cracking earth. His webbed feet hurt, and no matter how much he attempts to keep clean, his feathers always seem dusty. He quacks halfheartedly and his days are without joy.

Then the rains come. Little streams trickle together, and puddles form. Soon the duck pond is full again, and excitedly the duck enters the water. He splashes the dust from his feathers, and his webbed feet pull him through the water swiftly and graciously. He is being his potential now. This is the life he was meant to live. He glories in his duckness.

So it is with the actualizing person. He has the sense of fully living. Exercising the ultimate in courage, he has performed the ethical act of affirming his own being, and life has become a dance.

Chapter VI
Toward an Actualization-Centered Church

A minister, seeking to build an actualizing church, puts the quest in perspective:

> We are looking for a place
>   where we can exercise trust in depth;
>   where listening, receiving, and giving
>   take place in a Communion.
> We are looking for a place
>   of genuine significance and identity,
>   where life and people and vocation
>   can be seen and experienced in proper perspective.
> We are looking for a place
>   where acceptance isn't earned by donning masks,
>   where relationships are genuine,
>   where struggle and faith are valid.
> We long for a place
>   which equips us together,
>   for each other and for all others,
>   to be alive in His life.
> We are looking for a place

where rich discipleship and experiments in faith
bring us to the moment of truth
when we say the "Yes" that counts!
We are looking for a place
where silly, stupid, subtle religious images
are challenged, surrendered, changed
and placed at His feet where they belong!
We are looking for a place
where the Person of Jesus Christ
and every person
can receive, from us, proper significance!
Where is that place?
We are looking for a place like that, Jesus! [1]

Is there such a place? We have caught glimpses of it, however faint, as we have sought to move toward Christian actualization in our churches. We have seen it in the relationships
of other congregations when the principles of actualization,
though unnamed and perhaps unknown, were put into
practice. One person found it and wrote of her experiences.

Perhaps for the first time in my life I was able to see myself, and
I didn't like all I saw. I went to the group thinking I was a "con-
fident Christian," only to discover that I was, instead, rather smug
and distant, more concerned with myself than with others. The
warmth and love for one another that soon enveloped the entire
group enabled me to shed this cocoon I had wrapped myself in,
and I finally started to grow, both as a person and as a Christian.

We are looking for a place like that, but we realize that we
will never find it unless in our own lives we can be the kind

[1] Hal Edwards, "We Are Looking for a Place."

of persons and practice a style of life that will set the stage for such a place to be realized.

Though we have been on this path deliberately for a short time, certain patterns have emerged that are worth sharing. Again, we don't have a recipe, nor can we talk about an institutional pattern in any fixed organizational sense. We *can* talk about institutional patterns that are dynamic and changing and about a style for the congregational life, as we have talked about a style for individuals.

In the previous chapter we noted that while we have our own *élan*, Jesus is our *élan vital*. We also noted that through our ultimate commitment to life as we find it revealed in him, the style of the Christian actualizing person takes form. One, we discover our potential; two, our relationships are transformed; three, we make our unique contribution. The church can provide the setting and the relationships for this individual style to be realized, nurtured, and developed. Here we see some emerging patterns that claim our attention as we move toward an actualization-centered church.

Worship: We Discover Our Potentials

Whatever structure the church takes, worship must be a dynamic part of its life. Here the three levels of awareness—self and self, self and others, self and God—are cultivated and celebrated. Here we discover our potentials as persons as we seek to explore the mighty ranges, the heights and depths, of the human spirit. We seek to loose these forces as we are empowered by the ultrapersonal experience of worship. C. G. Jung once observed that "everyone's ultimate aim and strongest desire lie in developing the fullness of human existence

115

that is called personality"—a goal, as he points out, to be realized through the establishment of a personal relation with a power outside ourselves.

AWARENESS

> We long for a place
> which equips us together,
> for each other and for all others,
> to be alive in His Life.

Awareness and the cultivation of it are two of the chief ends of worship. Louise Lavelle described the particular genius of the saints as their ability to "lend inwardness to whatever event they meet." This is the depth of awareness that is cultivated in worship—an inwardness that experiences the many levels of reality. In our submission to the manipulative tentacles of our culture the latent potentialities of consciousness remain buried, or at best clumsily expressed. This is what Erich Fromm calls the "hypnotic passivity" of modern man.

This awareness is not only a recognition of a power outside ourselves; it is a heightened sensitivity to the intrapersonal and the interpersonal experiences of the worshiper. We are equipped together for each other and for all others. "To be alive in His life" becomes a central act in actualizing worship. Samuel Miller calls the minister to operate with integrity as a celebrant in leading people in worship. "In the midst of this age, in the maelstrom of history in all its fury, in the muddled mess of this world, in the confusion and boredom and amazement, he ought to be able to . . . pick out a glory to celebrate. There should be something somewhere hidden in the common day, by the plain speech of a plain man, to break the sky asunder, to ascend on high in song." [2]

But not only is the minister or the priest to be celebrant. He is but one among many celebrants as the entire congregation experiences the unity of the intrapersonal, the interpersonal, and the ultrapersonal with the natural and man-made order.

Celebration, then, is the exclamation of good news that life is to be affirmed. Our essential business is not to bemoan the human predicament, but to celebrate the good news.

COMMUNITY

> We are looking for a place
>   of genuine significance and identity,
>   where life and people and vocation
>   can be seen and experienced in proper perspective.

What we are really looking for is community. O. Hobart Mowrer has suggested that the popularity of existentialism and the ubiquity of the question "Who am I?" indicate that we are entering, or perhaps are well into, an identity crisis, a moral and spiritual void. "This verdict derives from a manifest deterioration of ethical standards, preoccupation with sensuality and materialism, 'waste-making,' and 'status-seeking,' and the increasing incidence of what is generally called mental illness and other expressions of personal instability and disorganization." [3] The answer to an identity crisis is a strong sense of community and commitment.

[2] *The Dilemma of Modern Belief* (New York: Harper & Row, 1963), p. 108.

[3] *The New Group Therapy* (Princeton: D. Van Nostrand Co., 1964), p. 14.

117

Actualizing worship provides this. Here we can confess our sins and shortcomings; we can experience in the fellowship the sense of forgiveness and acceptance; we can be inspired to make restitution; we can recover our self-respect and identity; we can discover our potential as persons as we move away from the disastrously individualistic, independent, and isolated stance that is too characteristic of our lives and find the unity and interdependence of community.

HONESTY

> We are looking for a place
>> where silly, stupid, subtle religious images
>> are challenged, surrendered, changed
>> and placed at His feet where they belong!

The images, language, forms, and symbols of worship must be honest. Actualization calls us to live fully in the now. Worship that calls the worshiper to retire from this world into the "other" world is a perversion.

What happens in worship must be understandable outside worship. No hocus-pocus liturgy comprehended only by an inner circle will fill this purpose. In religion, as well as in other areas, we have our specialized jargon. Too often, especially in the church, this jargon is used as a crutch when communication is too difficult to wrestle with. No service of worship should ever conceal the faith and meaning of life in language that cannot be understood by today's reader of the daily newspaper.

The dawning recognition of this is seen in the growth of lay academies which, among other things, search for the meaning of worship and new ways in which worship can be celebrated—the introduction of folk music, drama, and art into worship services, the experimentation with dialogue sermons, new orders of worship, modern liturgies, and different avenues of congregational participation. The presence of Duke Ellington and his band in the chancels of cathedrals and of Sister Mary Corita, a Roman Catholic nun pop-artist, in the pulpits of Protestant churches indicates a deliberate effort on the part of some to find images, forms, and language that will communicate and assist in the celebration of life.

We bring to worship our real being in a degree of honesty as deep as possible. Here we sharpen our commitments, deepen our sensitivity, test our self-interests and self-concepts, and examine our loves in relation to the image of reality—our ultrapersonal experience of God.

Scorn Not Preaching

Each Sunday in the United States over 200,000 sermons are preached! Since the worship experience on Sunday mornings is the primary involvement of most Christians today, and for many their only relationship to the church, it is important that an actualizing style be developed specifically in relation to preaching.

There is a tendency in the "renewal movement" of the church to minimize preaching. Some are even suggesting that we get rid of it altogether. We *have* sometimes used it as a technique of manipulation, and the manipulating minister has found in it a false ego-strengthening crutch which he has used in an authoritarian way. Yet, when rightly understood and practiced, preaching can be an actualizing expression on the part of the entire congregation and the minister. Certainly it can be one of the finest stimulations to actualizing on the part of worshipers.

Howard J. Clinebell, Jr. says:

The sermon offers a minister one of his most valuable opportunities to enhance the mental and spiritual health of his people. Like group counseling, effective preaching offers an efficient means of helping a number of individuals simultaneously. From a mental health viewpoint, the sermon has both preventive and therapeutic potentialities. For relatively healthy persons it can stimulate personality growth and raise the general level of creativity. It can release strength within those who are struggling with a personal crisis. It can support those whose personality foundations are weak, and motivate some who are burdened to seek professional help.[4]

When we begin to understand preaching in this fashion and work to this end, it can be an actualizing experience for preacher and hearer.

Dialogue with and redemptive involvement in the lives of people are essential if preaching is to have a significant place in the actualization-centered church. If the minister has walked with troubled persons on their inner journeys and if members of the congregation have shared in one another's lives, then preaching will be deepened by the feeling for human problems.

In his preaching as in his total life the solemn responsibility of the minister is to enter into and sustain the I-thou relationship with his hearers. Since this is the way God himself ap-

---

[4] *Mental Health Through Christian Community* (Nashville: Abingdon Press, 1965), pp. 77-78.

proaches men and women, ministers cannot permit themselves to lose sight of it. Preaching, then, becomes *personal encounter*.

The actualizing preacher presents a *claim* and a *possibility*, and the hearer is free to respond. He can accept or reject. In this there is a personal encounter through the vehicle of speech, and all the ingredients of an actualizing relationship are present: honesty, awareness, freedom, and trust.

In light of this it is our conviction that the place of the sermon in worship does not need to be minimized. It needs to be made authentic. It is authentic when it presents a claim and a possibility to persons who are free in their response, and as a result of the confrontation of claim and possibility with will, shared meaning results. Herbert H. Farmer has discussed this adequately in *The Servant of the Word*. His contention is that the necessity for a community of insight and understanding, for shared meaning which comes through preaching, is an essential part of the personal, the I-thou world.

So the goal of preaching is to open new doors, provide new insights, shed more light, and offer *alternative courses of action*. Above all, hearers should be called to make a definite response—definite, but free.

D. T. Niles calls the minister to his task in preaching when he says:

The preacher is not a performer, he is a witness; and somehow a connection must be established between him and those to whom he witnesses. He must belong to their world and they to his. It is said of Father Damien that he began his Sunday sermon to the lepers among whom he lived with these words: "My Brethren."

One Sunday his opening words were, "We lepers." He had entered their world.[5]

Using Niles's figure of speech here, we would say that the minister who mistakenly sees himself as a performer is monological in his preaching. The one who sees himself as a witness is dialogical and actualizing. Reuel L. Howe, in *The Miracle of Dialogue,* talks of the "monological illusion." This is the erroneous belief that communication occurs when people are told what they ought to know. From his work at the Institute of Advanced Pastoral Studies, he concludes that many younger ministers are disillusioned with preaching because they are not aware of alternatives to the ineffective, homiletical monologue.[6]

We are not suggesting here that in the worship service conversation has to take place between minister and people in the sense that he talks to them and they "talk back" to him in a verbal fashion. This may or may not be. We *are* suggesting that minister and laymen in an actualization-centered church spend more time in efforts at creative communication. Browne Barr of Berkeley has shown one approach to this by having laymen actually share in his sermon preparation each week.

As the people were leaving an actualization-centered church one Sunday, a member said, "That was a fine sermon; I was helped." The minister replied, "It was a sermon *we* preached." The member understood, for during the week they had struggled together over the issue confronted in the sermon. The "talking back" is the exchange that takes place in the

<hr>

[5] *The Preacher's Calling to Be a Servant* (New York: Harper & Brothers, 1959), p. 19.

[6] (New York: Seabury Press, 1963), p. 32.

contact of minister and people. It is *being with* the people in order that he may speak understandingly and redemptively to their situation.

The dialogical preacher is able to talk in terms of everyday feelings, habits, and inspirations—commonplace life situations. He is able to translate formulations of a theological or psychological nature because he *knows* his people; he *feels* with them.

Bishop William A. Quayle spoke a great word for us:

When this preacher comes to a Sunday in his journey through the week, people ask him, "Preacher-man, where were you and what saw you while the workdays were sweating at their toil?" And then of this preacher we may say reverently. "He opened his mouth and taught them, saying:" and there will be another though lesser Sermon on the Mount. And the auditors sit and sob and shout under their breath, and say with their helped hearts, "Preacher, saw you and heard you that? You were well employed. Go out and listen and look another week; but be very sure to come back and tell us what you heard and saw." [7]

So preaching in an actualization-centered church is an experience of "shared meaning." It comes only when there is core contact within the congregation and real dialogue takes place. Where there is no dialogue, "the people perish." No core relationships, no actualization!

Koinonia: Our Relationships Are Transformed

In his play *The Burnt Flower-bed* Ugo Betti has one of his characters say:

[7] *The Pastor-Preacher* (Cincinnati: Jennings & Graham, 1910), p. 371.

That's what's needed, don't you see. THAT! Nothing else matters half so much. To reassure one another. To answer each other. Perhaps only YOU can listen to me and not laugh. Everyone has, inside himself . . . a great, very important character! . . . Every man must be persuaded—even if he's in rags—that he's immensely, immensely important! Everyone must respect him; and make him respect himself too. They must listen to him attentively.[8]

There is here a common need of man to which the church must always seek to respond. In recent years the different types of small groups that have been cropping up in congregations across the country indicate an effort on the part of the church to do just that. Prayer groups, study groups, encounter groups, supportive groups—the list goes on and on—are all efforts to meet this need of man to belong, to be accepted, to be forgiven, to be respected and loved. Here genuine communion according to the measure of man's need is sought.

Koinonia has become the key word in describing the experience that is sought in this small-group movement. It is a New Testament Greek word describing the fellowship of the early Christians. It was not a spirit of fellowship, but a fellowship of the Spirit. By common need, common confession, common forgiveness, common acceptance, and common service, this fellowship became the force that amazed the first-century world. It is this kind of fellowship that we seek as we move toward an actualization-centered church.

REAL COMMUNION

> We are looking for a place
>   where we can exercise trust in depth;

[8] *Three Plays,* Henry Reed, trans. (New York: Grove Press, 1958), p. 151.

> where listening, receiving, and giving
> take place in a Communion.

A Christian actualization group (see suggestions for this in the next chapter) became such a place for a young lady. She came into the group several months after a nearly successful suicide attempt.

Through a variety of experiences the members of the group were encouraged to share their struggles and become present to each other in caring community. In one session members of the group were asked to draw a picture of some experience they had had or a feeling about themselves. The young woman drew a series of pictures.

"This is me before I understood I was worth loving." Here she presented a dejected figure against a heavy background of black with chaotic lines superimposed over the figure.

"Because I didn't love myself, I thought no one else cared. I tried to kill myself. In the picture I am attempting to commit suicide." Here she shared a picture of a girl with a bottle of poison.

"In this picture there are persons who saved me from destroying my body. You are all in this next picture because you have helped me to see that I am a worthwhile person who can have a meaningful life." The drawing here was of a group with smiling faces, lines indicating many-sided communications, and hands supporting one another.

"This next picture isn't very clear, and I don't exactly know what it means, but I'd like to think I'm discovering that God is not a mean old judge who's down on me for the bad things I've done, but one who cares for me and wants me to be well." Here was only an abstract burst of color.

"These last two pictures sort of sum up where I have been and where I am now." She presented a girl in a coffin and in contrast a girl in a flowery meadow at the foot of a mountain trail. "I see myself as being dead before, and alive now."

What is sought in the *koinonia* of an actualizing congregation is real communion, real contact between real persons. It involves personal commitment in a dialogue between two "cores" or real inner selfhoods of two actualizing persons. This always involves a trusting relationship of love and acceptance. In actualizing relationships the relationship is one of closeness, of touching. In manipulating relationships the relationship is one of distance and impersonal communication.

In Chapter IV we talked about the three levels of awareness: *intra*personal, *inter*personal, and *ultra*personal. These three levels of experience form the basis for communion, for communion is a three-way relationship: self and self, self and others, self and God. This trinity of relationships is essentially integrated. If one level is missing, the others are limited.

Man's spiritual communion with others is uniquely his. This is the difference between an individual and a person: the individual associates whereas the person communicates. And to use Paul Tournier's fine figure, this is the difference between the personage and the person: the personage is an external appearance which touches the personage of others from outside; the person communicates inwardly with the second person, the "thou."

This communion is a fragile thing and must be developed in each relationship at each meeting. When we experience it, we feel a transparency of relationship; we invite others into our most intimate world, and we enter into theirs. With most people this kind of contact is rare and difficult to establish. The more actualizing we are, the easier and more natural it becomes. One experience of communion equips us for the possibility of other experiences, upon which we are constantly building.

Genuine relationships are experienced on a one-to-one basis and are possible primarily in small groups. As we move toward an actualization-centered church, we seek to provide various opportunities for communion in these groups. To be effective the participants must understand that they must be honest and open—as transparent as possible. This always involves risk. Instead of controlling, as we do in manipulative relationships, we leave ourselves vulnerable to judgment, exposed to harsh reality as conceived by others—but above all, we reveal the dimensions of ourselves that we have heretofore denied or refused to see. In this experience we receive forgiveness and are accepted. Thus the stage for change and growth is set. Everyone has the chance to remove the mask and confront the concerns that are important to him. This can be the "midnight hour," about which Kierkegaard spoke, "when we must all unmask." Core relationships—being with being, thou with thou, and thou with Thou—are possible here. Experiences are no longer casual and superficial, but deep and meaningful.

"We are looking for a place . . . where relationships are genuine, where struggle and faith are valid." There is a big question in our lives as we seek to be agents of love and concern, as we seek to lead others in the way of life that we have found in Christ: Is there some way to assist others in coming to this way more quickly and more easily than we have come? Obviously our paths have been illuminated by others who enabled us to choose one way or the other. But it took such a long time! Is it possible that we can do something or be something that will enable others to emerge sooner? Should we simply *be* with others to assuage their loneliness in their time of struggle, or by the transparency of our *being,* the revealing of ourselves, can we provide them light?

Bernard Martin answers our question with superb insight and sensitivity as he closes the record of his own spiritual pilgrimage in this direction: "I now realize that to heal a man includes more than protecting him from destruction. It is also to provide him with the possibility of pursuing his path, to lead him to progressive blossoming of his person, to return to him the capability of living. I also know that to accomplish this sacred task, one must himself be a living person, really and authentically." [9] In *koinonia,* "where relationships are genuine, where struggle and faith are valid," we are led and we lead others to a progressive blossoming of their personhood. The capability of living is restored. Guilt and forgiveness, our most basic concerns and topics which are central in the church's proclamation, are faced and experienced. The clamoring question of the possibility of human existence is raised, and beyond that, the possibility of being fully human and fully Christian is confronted.

CONVERSATIONS: ON A BARSTOOL, AT CHURCH

A minister, seeking to lead his congregation in genuine concern and love for the individual, wrote a column in his weekly bulletin entitled "Conversations: On a Barstool, at Church" which puts this movement toward *koinonia* in perspective:

[9] *If God Does Not Die,* J. H. Farley, trans. (Richmond: John Knox Press, 1966), p. 79.

Many a nagging wife wonders what her husband finds in a bar that he can't find at home! And many fellows wonder why some men go to church when they can sit on a barstool and engage in conversation with real people. Going to the bar gets you closer to people than going to church, they say.

You go to the bar to talk, to say exactly what you feel. You can use all the four-letter adjectives you need to get your point across. Nobody will condemn you; you are free to fail; you can admit your passions, your guilt, your loneliness, your problems, your sins. The great high priest (bartender) is a good listener. You go home with a listened-to feeling.

Where is the church where you can get that listened-to feeling? Where is the church that gives a man acceptance, gut-level acceptance, regardless of the skin or the problem or the need or the sin? Who are those church members who possess enough honesty to admit their need and their sins?

We at St. Mark's can learn something from the local bar, you know! How can we blame a man for going to a bar where he is usually listened to—for quite a nominal fee?

Getting that Sunday morning smile and a shallow "Well, hello! It's good to see you" just isn't enough!

If we let the Holy Spirit make us a church with power in this community, we will of necessity discover the everlasting individual and give him the chance to get a real experience of Christ and in meaningful conversations come to the place where he has the freedom to be honest. But he cannot have that kind of freedom unless we put our honesty forward first—and church people don't usually come that honest! We like to put only the good forward; we are heretics in the game of truth. The sooner we discover the need to communicate on the one-to-one the sooner we become the church of Jesus Christ. To do that we must listen in depth and be deeply influenced by the consciousness of Christ, who hates sin and loves the sinner.

Mission: We Make Our Unique Contribution

We are looking for a place
where rich discipleship and experiments in faith
bring us to the moment of truth
when we say the "Yes" that counts!

Actualizing worship and *koinonia* enable us to celebrate the three levels of our experience and lead us into "rich discipleship and experiments in faith." Actualizing worship brings us to the moment of truth when we say "Yes" to life.

In Jackson, at the height of the racial tension in Mississippi in September, 1963, the following advertisement appeared in the leading daily newspaper:

THE FIRST ——————————— CHURCH
takes pleasure in announcing the installation of a

NEW STREET-LEVEL ELEVATOR

This modern installation will be operational beginning
September 29

There followed some instructions giving directions to the entrance of the elevator. Then came the clincher. Across the bottom of the advertisement in bold letters were the words:

THERE ARE NO STEPS TO CLIMB IF YOU WORSHIP WITH US

Not far from that church, Sunday after Sunday, police stood guard. When ushers of the church and others of the

130

city turned "unsuitable people" away from the church doors, the police would arrest the turned-away people for disturbing public worship.

While the advertisement may have been literally and symbolically true of the church in Jackson, it can never be even symbolically true of an actualizing congregation. There are steps to climb, and often they are arduous ones. In worship and in *koinonia* the confrontation that is ours at the three levels of our experience calls us to greater and deeper involvement in life and in the world. Yet this involvement is always one of free response. It must never be coercion by the church, nor should it be the drudgery of "keeping the law," but rather the free movement of a person who responds to life and accepts responsibility for life. To evade this response and responsibility is fatal. It means self-defeat for the person and for the congregation. The noted historian of Greece, Edith Hamilton, stated the challenge as she wrote of the decline of Athens, "When the freedom they wished for most was freedom from responsibility, then Athens ceased to be free and was never free again."

About the same time that the advertisement of the church in Mississippi proclaimed "There are no steps to climb if you worship with us," the Conference of Church Leaders of the German Democratic Republic issued "Ten Articles of Freedom and Service in the Church." It was one of the most courageous actions taken by organized religion in modern times. The statement was issued by the church in East Germany in the midst of the control policies of the Communist regime. The first paragraph points the direction for the actualizing church: "Jesus sent his church into the world in order that it proclaim

131

to all people the reconciliation of God and bear witness to God's will in all areas of life. He who accepts the word of God will not have to live under oppressive coercion, but will attain a glorious freedom." This bold statement was closed with this affirmation of hope:

In this confidence, the Christian community will help, as far as this is possible, to overcome the sufferings and needs in this world and to put something better in the place of the worse. It knows that all human endeavor is temporary and lacks perfection. It is waiting for the day when what it believes even today will be manifest before all the world.

Involvement in life and the world characterizes the actualization-centered church. To become aware of and to celebrate the three levels of our experience in worship and *koinonia* lead us to daily involvements in the life of people where we are to function as agents of loving reconciliation.

A sort of heart-hardening has set in upon most of us. Though more and more we are coming to be a "welfare state" and, on the face of it, such a state is built upon the foundation of human caring, there is still a disturbing atrophy of the human spirit. In one of the chapters of his book *Grace and the Searching of Our Heart* Charles R. Stinnette, Jr., has asked a scathing question: "Who cares in a world of caretakers?" He makes a penetrating commentary on the caretaker attitude:

The truth is that where the caretaker attitude prevails, man is reduced to a cipher. His needs are supplied, but human response is neither given nor evoked. In such a climate it appears that the food or good which one is able to provide by the wizardry of his technology becomes a kind of magic which is substituted for human concern which might have been given. The personhood of both the dispenser and the recipient is robbed by such an attitude. Indeed, the responsible person is prevented from ever reaching maturity. The person becomes a commodity, and his eternal soul acquires a price tag.[10]

One of the deepest needs in life is to care lovingly, and this loving care must be communicated personally and intimately. To be cared for is an equally deep need and cannot be satisfied except by personal involvement. Our own humanity is defaced if we do not respond.

FOCUS AND SPONTANEITY

Increasingly we are learning that we must reject trying to do everything and focus upon what is most needed at the moment. As a symbol of this understanding the leaders of one Christian actualization group begin their meetings in this way: holding the Bible in one hand and the newspaper in the other, the leader says, "Brothers, God is speaking to us through these sources. Let us hear and respond to what God is saying."

The story of the flood in San Felipi, Mexico (September, 1967), was read by people in this group. Their response was spontaneous. They mobilized the community and within a few days truckloads of clothing and food were on the way to this washed-out fishing village. The world and the Word determined the mission of the church.

[10] (New York: Association Press, 1962), p. 46.

At the heart of the gospel is another word as important as the word *koinonia*. It is *diakonia*. Originally it was a word without glamor and must have meant something like "serving at tables." The New Testament provides a series of variations on one theme: here was one who came not to be served, but to serve. He was "the man for others," though he also appreciated the gracious service of others. That Jesus came not to be served is nothing new; that idea can be found almost any place. But that he deliberately came to serve—this is fresh and unique.

So the word *diakonia* indicates the pattern of life of those who would follow Jesus. They are servants. They are other-directed. The three levels of awareness become more in balance in their life. For them the eternal power game holds no charm. They move toward ceasing to dominate, to control, and to manipulate. Even without deliberation they find themselves ministering to others and always seem to be available wherever there is need.

Historically the same thing has happened to this concept of *diakonia* in the church as has happened to the "caretaker" concept in modern society. J. C. Hoekendijk in *The Church Inside Out* has capsuled this deterioration of meaning in a cryptic way:

This is what also happened to the deacon. He entered the tunnel as a waiter, only to come out as an assistant to the bishop— a near-priest. He had been neatly clericalized. He had been removed from behind the backs of the table guest and been placed somewhere at the head of the table. And that is where he still sits in our churches, as a respectable displaced person. The intentions were no doubt good. In the meantime, the effects were fatal. The deacon moved from the street, where he belonged, to the altar space and the front bench, where from then on he would only symbolize service. The solidarity became spiritualized, detached from the sphere of direct physical contact. When we behold the dress of deacons (the dalmatic among the Catholics and the black suits in many Protestant churches), it becomes immediately apparent that here only the depiction of an idea is meant. In this uniform no one will recognize the livery of people who are available, ready to do some down-to-earth labor.[11]

The actualization-centered church must seek to recover for modern man the concept of *diakonia,* the idea of spontaneous service. Again, freedom is the key word. To simply program this service or to outline its procedure and methodology will kill the spirit and bring into bondage again that which is most valid when it is performed without conditions. "Truly, I say to you, as you did it to one of the least of these my brethren," said Jesus, "you did it to me." In service—service to the least, performed in spontaneous, unprogrammed, unsuspected, uncalculated ways—we gain the ultimate freedom: freedom from self.

Not only must we see ourselves as servants of others, we must be actualizing as was Jesus in *receiving* the ministry of others. We have discovered that many Christians are uneasy and even have real guilt feelings when they are the recipients rather than the givers of gifts. While the statement of Jesus, "It is more blessed to give than to receive," is true, paradoxically it is also true that it is more difficult to receive than to give.

[11] (Philadelphia: The Westminster Press, 1966), pp. 148-49.

The actualizing Christian has his polarities in balance: giving and receiving are natural expressions of his style. "She has done a beautiful thing," Jesus said of the woman who "wasted" costly perfume on his feet. He was a gracious receiver as well as a gracious giver.

We are speaking of many gifts here: understanding, appreciation, acceptance, concern, comfort. The person who says "It was nothing" when he has given himself to another is a thief. He robs himself of the joy of receiving the gratitude and appreciation of another, and in turn robs the other of the fulfillment that could have come from expressing his true feelings of thankfulness. So we minister by giving and by receiving.

This, then, is the rhythm of the actualizing church: worship, *koinonia, diakonia.* Worship should have the characteristics of *koinonia,* but perhaps more important in our day of "big" churches, worship should inspire the worshiper to find the place where *koinonia* may be experienced. *Koinonia,* in turn, makes one sensitive to his need to return to the community of worshipers and also to move out in involvement in mission. *Diakonia,* entered into by free response, becomes the expression of accepted responsibility on the part of the congregation and the individual. Involved in *diakonia,* the person senses more keenly the need for the inspiration and strength that are gained in worship and *koinonia.* So the pattern of the actualizing congregation is incomplete unless opportunities for these three experiences are provided. The rhythmic life of the individual within an actualizing congregation is one of movement among these three expressions of one's commitment: worship, *koinonia, diakonia.*

We are looking for a place
>   where the Person of Jesus Christ
>   and every person
>   can receive, from us, proper significance!
Where is that place?
>   We are looking for a place like that, Jesus!

The place is everywhere, but nowhere unless in us!

Chapter VII
The Christian Actualization Group

In *Man, the Manipulator* the problem and the alternatives of manipulation and actualization for modern man were set forth. In the previous chapters of this book this problem and alternatives have been seen in the context of the church. A crucial question now is, Can a person traverse the continuum from manipulation to actualization? If so, how?

In *Man, the Manipulator* the inner journey to personal actualization was presented. In this volume we are describing this method as it is practiced in the context of the Christian church. The continuum can be traversed, as we have witnessed in our own experience. One primary vehicle for the journey is the Christian actualization group. The idea of such a group is not a new thing. It is as old as the church.

A quick survey of the Christian church verifies this. The early church, in its dynamic, was a small-group movement akin to some of our modern small-group efforts. The common commitment of the group resulted in honest sharing at the level of the best group therapy of today. Personal confession and honest encounter were a primary part of the community.

So unique in this respect was the early church that the Greek word *koinonia* best characterizes it.

This *koinonia* way of life—the spirit of loving, caring, and sharing, which we talked about in the preceding chapter—was the dimension that gave the early church its strong personal impact. It was this kind of life, which found expression in exuberance and joy and love, that was so novel and arresting. Those who observed the early Christians could not understand it, and some said, "See how these men love one another."

With the growth of the church, the institutionalizing of it (the cessation of public and the introduction of private confession), and the formalizing of worship, this powerful dimension of *koinonia* was lost to a great degree. O. Hobart Mowrer in *The New Group Therapy* suggests that the impact of group therapy in modern-day psychology and the growth and dynamic of communism in its "cell" structure are results of this loss.

We are suggesting here that the modern church, if it is to develop again the spirit that characterized the early church, must again recover this way of *koinonia*, this way of intimacy and sharing, by having actualization-centered groups akin to those of the early church. For us today *koinonia* is at least the integration of the spirit of actualization into the total church. The three levels of awareness—the intrapersonal, the interpersonal and the ultrapersonal—are lived out in relationships.

The small-group movement in the church has gained momentum during the past ten years. The Christian actualization group is an effort on our part to add to this momentum and to experiment with ways of adding meaning and depth to it.

While the Christian actualization group is not an effort to bring group therapy into the church, it is a deliberate attempt to use the process of group dynamics to wed the unique functions of minister and psychologist for the purpose of valuing, self-discovery, and self-commitment. Though our most fruitful experiences have come when minister and therapist have worked together, this is not to preclude growth in actualization in any group wherever certain dynamics of relationships are responded to. Here, however, the dynamics of the Christian actualization group is our concern.

The Beginning of a Christian Actualization Group

Christian actualization groups begin as a result of ministers and laymen feeling the need to recover the *koinonia* aspect of the church. In our experience such groups began as a result of a close personal and professional relationship. Sensing the possibility of this dynamic for the life of the church, we extended invitations from the pulpit for people to experiment in such a relationship.

In any church such groups may be formed, using as resources this book and *Man, the Manipulator* along with other resources that will be listed in the "Further Help" section of the book. The invitation should make clear the purpose of the group.

When those who respond come together, something like the following introduction may be made:

The minister may describe the spirit of *koinonia* that characterized the early church as members met together in small groups. The constituency of the group will determine how extensive this will be. A clear word should be spoken about

140

the fact that this is not just an effort to bring psychology into the church but is an attempt to bring to present-day experience the vitality of the early church. The psychologist may be introduced as one who would assist in leading the actualization group.

The psychologist would then outline some of the basic rules for the actualization group. A mimeographed sheet should be prepared and given to each person. Introducing these, the psychologist might say: "Basically, we would like you to attend to two principles: (1) Make all your expressions in the here and now. Don't talk about the past or the future; talk only about what you feel is going on inside you now. Be absolutely honest with one another. What you feel on the inside, say. The key phrase is WIGO—What Is Going On—be sure to share what you feel is going on. (2) Speak only about your feelings, not your ideas. This is not a philosophy group. We want to be experience-centered and talk only about how we *feel* about ourselves and how we *feel* about others in the group."

After such an introduction, the group usually has little or no trouble expressing itself. The group meets weekly, and at the beginning of each meeting the leader will summarize what has taken place in the previous meetings, the direction the group seemingly is seeking to go, and ask for response to it. He will encourage the group to relate to one another on the basis of expressed needs. Always the characteristics of manipulation and actualization are focused upon. This is adequate stimulation for the full function of the group.

The functions of the minister and psychologist will be described later in this chapter.

Guides for the Christian Actualization Group

There are many churches where it is impossible for a psychologist and a minister to work together in leading a group. It is possible for groups without this kind of leadership to function in an actualizing way. Group leadership training is available through private psychologists, universities, and centers like the Institute of Therapeutic Psychology in Santa Ana, California.[1]

On the West Coast particularly *sensitivity training*, which equips leaders of groups, is available. The small sensitivity training group provides an opportunity to experience yourself more fully in your relations with others. The goal is to get a more accurate image of yourself as an instrument in interpersonal relations in order to free yourself to function more effectively in those relations, without being excessively burdened by unrealistic assumptions about your personal adequacy, your worth, or your social acceptability.

Not too unlike the Christian actualization group in its dynamics, sensitivity training provides the opportunity to

> learn more about yourself and your impact on others;
> understand your own feelings and how they affect your behavior toward others;
> become more sensitive to the ways people communicate with each other;
> learn "active listening"—for meanings and for feelings;

[1] A number of books like *Therapeutic Psychology—Principles of Actualization Counseling and Psychotherapy,* by Lawrence M. Brammer and Everett L. Shostrom (2nd. ed.; Englewood Cliffs, N.J.: Prentice-Hall, 1968), are available. Also, a film series entitled "The Actualization Group" is available from the Institute of Therapeutic Psychology. See the "Further Help" section, p. 170.

learn how people affect groups and groups affect people;
learn how to help groups function more effectively.[2]

In our experience certain fundamental principles have enabled groups to function in an actualizing way. These principles, along with the content of this chapter, help individuals involve themselves on the *feeling* level and can be used in any group process. They are:

1. Always use "I," never "them, they, we, you, us," etc.—"I feel," "I think," "I am."
2. Avoid "but," "although," "because"—"I feel hurt today," *not* "because I was hurt by my husband." "I don't like you," *not* "but I don't like people like you."
3. Attempt to verbalize your feelings and thoughts in the here-and-now situation. Even past and future experiences should be expressed in the present—"I feel tense," *not* "I was driving here tonight and felt terrible." Feel terrible now!
4. When addressing a fellow group member, talk to him directly, eye-to-eye contact, and *don't* use third person when relating to him—"I like you," *not* "I like him."
5. Be constantly aware of what your body wisdom is saying to you. Listen to your tensions, boredom, joys, etc., and communicate these to the group. This is best done by listening to your voice.
6. When you are spoken to, listen intently to what is said and with what feeling it is being expressed. Some people only listen. Try to *hear* and *listen*.
7. The one question that should not be asked is "Why?" For example, if someone expresses caring for you, please

[2] From the UCLA sensitivity training brochure.

don't ask why! Be responsive to the other person. How do you feel when this person cares for you?

What usually happens in the group is described in a later section of this chapter entitled "The Process of Awareness." But first we look at the role of the therapist and minister.

The Role of the Therapist and Minister

The therapist is trained to observe and describe the various patterns of manipulation or neurotic interaction that take place between members of the group. The minister acts as a catalyst for confession and expression on the part of the group members and also provides a value frame of reference. Encouraging self-disclosure or confession of misdeeds or guilts is also important. But both minister and psychologist must also be willing to disclose themselves as persons and not as "professionals" detached from the group. In order for the minister to be this participant-observer, training is required, and such training is being made available today. The emphasis of actualization groups is on helping persons to change, but this change is a continuous process and not a once-and-for-all one as in earlier concepts of conversion. Each meeting of the group is a new opportunity for a different form of rebirth.

In a Christian actualization group both the minister and psychologist are present. These men make their unique contributions to the business of valuing.

A major premise is that actualization groups "value the process of valuing." A value we define as an emotionally charged idea to which an individual commits himself. All persons have either implicit or explicit values, and the purpose of the actualization group is to help each person clarify, refine, and make more explicit his value system. A minister, in effect, is a proclaimer of values. A psychologist is an evaluator of values. All values need to be tested against five existing frames of reference.

1. *Organismic.* For example, in Christian actualization groups a person may say, "But I don't get angry." Then the therapist or minister may say, "You say that you are not angry about being challenged, and yet your fists show that you *are* angry." Here one's organism (body) is used as the criterion for testing the validity of his declared values.

2. *Scientific.* "You say that you believe that you shouldn't express strong feelings, and yet science shows that if you don't, you can develop psychosomatic symptoms." We seek always to help persons examine the myths by which they live.

3. *Societal.* "You say that you don't believe in divorce, and yet our society today readily accepts divorce." Here we put into focus conflicts in society which all must face.

4. *Group.* "You say that you are always kind, and yet the group concurs that you are often hostile and angry." The group becomes a mirror of what one really is.

5. *Spiritual.* "You say that you are glad that you are humble, but Jesus said that you must be careful not to become proud of your humility."

The goal of the Christian actualization group is to create self-expression of the person and to help him grow in the valuing process.

The dynamics of the group have to do with the process of reevaluating and expanding the values of an individual. The minister is able to proclaim religious values and to help reinterpret values which are presently held. The psychologist examines manipulative and neurotic assumptions. No values are accepted as self-evident and axiomatically true. Many of us have accepted values as a result of expediency or accidents or because of slavish identification with others whom we have admired or hated during our lives. In the Christian actualization group there are no "sacred cows." Thus value evaluation requires intensive analysis of ideas which have been held uncritically in the past. It requires that the individual veritably chew over these ideas until they have become personally meaningful.

The psychologist and the minister are more like resource persons than answer givers. Group members are encouraged to risk disagreeing and expressing values of their own rather than simply agreeing with the values of the minister or psychologist. The task of the minister and psychologist is to create a situation of freedom where individuals are encouraged to respond freely rather than to regurgitate ideas which have been given them or feelings that are considered safe and appropriate by other authorities. Out of this a personal value system will develop. It will not be a finished product, but will be developmental in the sense that it will remain open to the changing values of the person as he grows and understands the issues of life more deeply. This leads to personal commitment as the individual develops awareness of his value system.

The minister and psychologist consciously and deliberately seek to avoid threats or demands or leading. Rather, each expresses personal values and encourages others to do the same. Therefore, the purpose of the group is: (1) to describe values and behaviors which seem to be held and practiced implicitly by the members, (2) to view these ideas and behaviors over against certain alternatives, and (3) to discover inconsistencies in currently held values and behaviors.

The process of the Christian actualization group is to help each person become increasingly aware of himself. This is not achieved by lectures or preaching. Awareness is an *experience*, not an *explanation*. Becoming-aware is never fully achieved. It is like the effort to climb the mountain of truth. None of us ever reach the top, but the joy of living is in the seeking, not the attainment.

The Process of Awareness

The process of actualization therapy can be thought of as a progression in awareness. In the context of the church this progression moves through three levels of awareness: self and self, self and others, self and God. The following is a description of the process in its dynamic.

CONFRONTING THE SELF

In the Christian actualization group therapist and minister first of all observe. As each person talks, he expresses a pattern which may be described as his style of life. For example, a person in a group may demonstrate his attempt at Christianity in one or two major ways: by being *active* or *passive*. The active Christian may take the stance of the *heavy*, attempting to dictate to other members of the group what is "right." He may become the *critic*, judging the church, others, and the minister. There is also the *calculator*, who schemes to maintain control of the group by conniving.

The passive Christian plays the reverse game. There is the *good* Christian, who always does what he is asked. There is the *humble* Christian, who depreciates himself and finds virtue in his unworthiness. There is the *protector*, who "sacrifices" himself unselfishly for the good of others—always giving but never asking. There is the *clinging vine,* who sits helplessly by, waiting to be fed and taken care of by the church. ("Oh, Reverend, you don't know how much I need you and the church!")

Working corporately, the psychologist and minister observe and describe the manipulative patterns. Each person in the group is confronted with his individual self-defeating pattern.

Looking back upon this "forced" confrontation, one person wrote:

I still tend to act God-like, feeling that although I might be helping some people, I am hurting others. I tend to take the responsibility for other people's feelings and behavior. But the actualization experience has made me aware that I do this. There now exists the possibility that I can do something about it. . . . Without this awareness, there could be no hope of change and no growth.

It is important to note here the indispensable function of the persons and skills of both the minister and the psychologist. Some Christians use self-righteousness as a defense. Confronting the psychologist only, the Christian finds it easy to run behind the wall of his interpretation of Christian teaching and escape confrontation with the sin of his self-righteousness.

For example, two brothers were in a Christian actualization group. The younger brother had asked his older brother to view his recent work on television. The TV programs involved interpersonal relationships. Rather than appreciating the significance of the work, the older brother chose instead to play the self-righteous judge and condemned his brother for not making a "Christian witness" to this wide audience. He felt virtuous for his ardent evangelistic spirit.

In the context of the group, however, the minister confronted him with his callous indifference to the needs of the younger brother and his failure to see and appreciate the implicit witness that was made. A psychologist alone might not have reached this man. The minister did. The older brother was willing to accept the minister's sharing concerning the validity of the young brother's witness.

An essential element here is timing. The older brother was caught in the act. In a sermon the principle would never have reached him since his self-concept precluded any guilt. But here he was confronted with his bare self.

As part of the process of confrontation an important function of the leaders is to assist members of the group in becoming aware of the neurotic gains they are obtaining from using manipulative styles or games. For example, active manipulations have a coercive controlling value—the payoff is that a sense of power is achieved by playing the "top-dog." The lay person who plays the "deacon" in the church (assigned or assumed) gets a great sense of power from his presumed superiority over other members of the group. The psychologist and minister in their confrontation help him recognize and admit the feelings of glee he experiences when controlling others. It is *very important* that the person become aware of the short-range payoff of his manipulative tendencies.

In contrast to the active manipulator the passive manipulator must be brought to see the short-range gain of his seductive manner. The "sweet mother of the Ladies Aid" whose motto is "service above self" must be confronted by her secret payoff

149

from her miserable martyrdom. Her theme song is, "I guess I just have to do everything around here; no one else seems to care." In the group she is asked, "What do you get from playing this game?" This may be the first time that she faces her secret feelings of righteous omnipotence. She must be confronted with them until she realizes that her gains from them are short-ranged and unfulfilling.

In real confrontation the manipulator sees that in the immediate present he does win a payoff, but in the long run he really loses by his self-defeating manipulations. As for the deacon, he must become aware of the distance between himself and others and the loneliness which results from his system. And the sweet mother must become aware of the shallow fulfillment and lack of intimate contact that comes from her busy work.

Many times change does not take place without causing embarrassment. In another day this may have been called conviction of sin.

For example, a wife is condemningly talking of her husband's infidelity. The psychologist insists that she play the role of the "judge" condemning him.

Wife: Repent! You know that you have committed adultery and have sinned against your wife and God. I'm going to see that you get your just punishment. I will see to it that you will not get away with it.

Psychologist: Could you substitute the word "grow" for "not get away with it?"

Dawning recognition comes as she realizes her own failure. The group in which this occurred realized that she saw herself as a condemning manipulative judge whose sole interest was retribution, rather than change. A sermon in this case would have been futile. Rather than being told the truth, the woman actually experienced it. *Change comes through experiences, not explanations.*

In restoring the inner balance, the expression of the opposite polarity is often necessary. After inwardly experiencing the foolishness of being the manipulative judge that she was, the woman was asked to play the "protector" and feel her responsibility for the sin of her husband in an extreme way. In playing this out, she said, "I hate to admit this, but I am responsible for your sin. I have had a lover, too. My lover was the League of Women Voters. Rather than being at home with you, I was out with my lover." Here the woman is exaggerating her guilt, yet this is sometimes necessary to bring the situation into perspective and restore the inner balance between the judge and the protector.

The fundamental idea here is that any exaggerated manipulation reveals the repression of its opposite. The deacon playing the dictator game may be covering up an unwillingness to face his softness and his need for tenderness. The "sweet martyr mother may be avoiding the expression of her needs to be aggressive and hostile. The clinging vine who depends so heavily on the church and the minister may be at a deeper level—the calculator who controls those who serve her. Her implicit message is, "By acknowledging your greatness I have the right to demand your services day or night."

Only when the individual within the group experiences these polarities is he ready for the final step in the process of awareness: *accepting conflict as a means of integration.*

Identifying Manipulative vs. Actualizing Polarities in the Actualization Group

The minister or psychologist can be aided in helping the group identify the various manipulative or actualizing polarities that are present by listening to the language that is expressed. The chart below is a summary of expressed verbalizations which are indicative of manipulative vs. actualizing patterns in dialogue. A further use for this summary is to test the understanding of the group members by having them fill in examples of their own manipulative or actualizing expressions.

We also suggest that this exercise be used only at the time when group members have achieved a sufficient sophistication in identification of manipulative and actualizing patterns. Enough sessions should have transpired so that the verbal patterns shown can be easily identified by group members.

MANIPULATING VS. ACTUALIZING DIALOGUE [3]

TOP-DOG STATEMENTS	POLAR UNDER-DOG RESPONSES
MANIPULATOR	
DICTATOR	WEAKLING
(1) You *have to*—or else!	(1) I'd love to, but I can't.
(1) You *can't*.	(2) You're right, but I *have to*.
(3) _____	(3) _____

[3] Copyright 1968 by the Institute of Therapeutic Psychology, Santa Ana, California.

152

ACTUALIZOR

LEADER
(1) I'd *like* you to.

(2) I *want* you to.

(3) _____

EMPATHIZER
(1) How do you want it done?
(2) Let's see how we can do it.
(3) _____

MANIPULATOR

CALCULATOR
(1) You'd better *or else*.
(2) I *know* what you're thinking.
(3) _____

CLINGING VINE
(1) If you say so.

(2) You're SO RIGHT!

(3) _____

ACTUALIZOR

RESPECTER
(1) I feel you'd profit by . . .
(2) I feel that you want . . .
(3) _____

APPRECIATOR
(1) I appreciate your concern.
(2) What I really want is. . .
(3) _____

MANIPULATOR

BULLY
(1) How stupid can you get!
Who do you think you are?
Don't be ridiculous!
(2) If you don't like it, you know what you can do.
(3) _____

NICE GUY
(1) I'm sorry.

(2) Please don't talk like that.
That hurts me.
(3) _____

ACTUALIZOR

ASSERTOR

(1) From my point of view. . .
As I see it . . .
(2) I feel very strongly about this.

(3) _____

CARER

(1) I'm interested in your ideas. Tell me more.
(2) I feel strongly too; I'd like to understand our differences.

(3) _____

MANIPULATOR

JUDGE

(1) It's all your (his) fault.
(2) You (he) should be ashamed of yourself himself).

(3) _____

PROTECTOR

(1) I (he) couldn't help it.
(2) Something came over me (him).

(3) _____

ACTUALIZOR

EXPRESSER

(1) I feel you are responsible.
(2) I feel you are wrong.

(3) _____

GUIDE

(1) You may be right; here's how I feel.
(2) How do you feel I'm wrong?

(3) _____

ACCEPTING CONFLICT AS A MEANS TO INTEGRATION

The goal of the group is to help a person realize that he need not reject his manipulative behavior. Traditionally some churches have said that one is to repress all negative attitudes and cease all negative behavior. This results in a constricting "don't-do-it-yourself" program and becomes bondage to law. Too often the expression of fears, doubts, and sin has had no

154

place in the life of those committed to Christianity. The expectation of manipulative religion has been that only joy, victory, and peace be the expressed message.

In the Christian actualization group conflict is appreciated and valued, rather than denied. The open awareness of one's manipulations is a major step to actualization. Once we are aware of the self-defeating nature of our manipulations, we begin to see the possibility of and the need to change. When we fall back into our manipulative patterns, we are even more sensitive to our plight of inner conflict. Paradoxically, *the accepting of the inner conflict between our self-defeating manipulations and our actualizing potentials is the way of integration.* Backsliding is accepted not as failure, but an inevitable part of a continuing process of growth.

One of the recent trends in psychotherapy has been to study the lives of self-actualized persons which are used as models of personal health. Maslow has suggested that studying the lives of men like Lincoln, Schweitzer, Gandhi and others of their caliber enables us to see the golden threads that make for full human functioning. In the Christian actualization group the primary model for actualization is Jesus. Christianity becomes most manipulative when dogma is made central. The actualization therapists of today are in the tradition of those who have championed person-centeredness. They help modern man recover the validity of a person-centered faith as opposed to a dogma-centered one.

In contrast to the self-actuali*zed* person who has achieved maximum effectiveness by common historical agreement, the actuali*zing* person is one who is moving toward personal fulfillment. One of the great values of group therapy in its best form is the association with self-actualizing persons who have achieved a measure of spiritual psychological health. In a Christian actualization group such people are "actualizing evangelists" who by their spontaneous expression and personal sharing provide inspiration for Christian growth. Implicit in the relationships of the group is the experience of acceptance and forgiveness which limits fear and provides freedom.

Dimensions of Involvement

A measure of the value of the Christian actualization group is the involvement that ensues. There are two primary dimensions of this involvement.

PERSONAL

When the group is fulfilling its function, the members are warm, human, and interested in one another. This requires objectivity about oneself and subjectivity in expression and relationship. Too often the church has not provided the actualizing experience necessary for escape from the octopus-like tenacles of manipulation because this personal element was missing.

When this is the case, the person in need of actualization finds himself a stranger among strangers. The Spirit acts in our actualization groups to unlock the doors, to free us from alienation and estrangement through personal relationships open to the Spirit's working.

By this experience we know that we are known and accepted by God as we are. The limiting fear of self-sharing is overcome; the need to remain hidden is eliminated. No longer do we need to pretend.

This kind of involvement does mean that each person in

such a group is in a position to hurt the others. And often real hurt is necessary before we can change. The wound has to be exposed before healing can come. The exposure of the wound is often the most painful experience.

AUTHENTIC CARING

The other essential dimension of involvement in the Christian actualization group is authentic caring. This we distinguish from the "love game" that characterizes so many of our superficial and phony relationships today, even some of our group relationships in the church.

"Pop culture" bombards us with music extolling "love" as the cure to all of life's problems. Novelists stress that lack of love causes racial discrimination, addiction, sodomy, and murder. Love is offered as the cure for war. Hugh Hefner's philosophy equates love with sex as does that of Helen Gurley Brown. Married men and women are given guilt feelings if they are not constantly "in love" twenty-four hours a day. Such false concepts of love cause more problems than they solve.

In the Christian actualization group authentic caring is substituted for these false concepts of love. This is done by replacing uncommitted casualness with intimate concern. Directness of expression, personal involvement, the shared power of hurting and healing—all characterize this relationship.

This authentic-caring kind of love expressed in the actualizing relationship is not to be misconstrued as something soft and undemanding. For love to be redemptive and therapeutic it has to be demanding and expectant. Also, it must be remembered that *active* love sometimes requires expression of angry and hostile feelings as well as warm and loving feelings. The actualization process requires that conflict, rather than simply passive acceptance, be a part of the process. It may be that this is the one principle that has been missing from the small-group movement of the church until now.

The Relationship of the Christian Actualization Group to Therapy and Evangelism

We would like now to relate the Christian actualization group first to the current group-therapy scene and then to evangelism or witnessing.

The Christian actualization group is not group therapy in the current sense of the word. In contrast to group therapy which is intended primarily for persons experiencing severe intrapersonal or interpersonal conflict, Christian actualization groups function for relatively healthy individuals who wish to improve their personal effectiveness and to function in a more authentic manner as Christians. Unlike sensitivity training and like groups designed to provide an experience for unselfconscious growth, the Christian actualization group is a self-conscious effort at growth in which the individual takes responsibility for his own development. The group also provides the setting where one's Christian commitment can be updated or an initial commitment can take place. Though the sharing of fulfillment and the confession of sin and failure, along with the experience of forgiveness, are important and of great impact, the emphasis in the Christian actualization group is primarily on *conscious intentions* and *actual behavior* in the present.

"The road to hell is paved with good intentions." "By

158

their fruits you shall know them." In relationships in the group we are measured by our actions, not our intentions. Increased awareness is the key to the possibility of change in our actions.

The second area to which we need to relate the Christian actualization group is evangelism. Our term for evangelism is Christian expression.

The church has sometimes proclaimed an evangelism which has been construed to mean planned, programmed, deliberate witnessing. Not always, but often, this has led to a practice of professional, manipulative witnessing. Witness of this type uses a technique which reduces the non-Christian to an *object*. Religion is "sold" as the proposed convert is manipulated into buying the product. Implicit in this technique is the motif of a top-dog convincing an inferior under-dog of his superior way of life.

Christian expression is an alternative to this model. The Christian actualization group is a setting where Christian expression is fostered and individuals are trained in spontaneous sharing. The result is the development of the "personal sharer" as opposed to the "professional witness."

The Group as an Instrument of Pastoral Care

One of the principles of the Christian actualization group is that pastoral care belongs to the entire church and not just to the ordained minister. All too often the minister has been placed in the role of *paid carer*. He has exclusive responsibility to minister to the sick, dying, and disturbed persons who come within the province of the church. This heresy has been proclaimed and practiced by the church until it is accepted as the proper mode of Christian ministry.

The actualization group helps move both minister and laity away from the one-man-show game that they have been playing. As the principles of actualization are lived out in the group, each member "moves from the need to receive ministry to the ability to give ministry as well." [4]

The actualization group helps to uncover the potential within many individuals in the church to really be agents of reconciliation and love. One of the significant discoveries in the pilot actualization groups is the recognition on the part of the minister that he is ministered to by the group and by individuals within it.

The Christian actualization group cares enough to encourage a person to be who he really is so that he can move on to what he should become. It is not rigid in its expectations of its members; it is not easily shocked or provoked. Its closeness springs not from a shallow level of conventionality, but from the rock-bottom honesty that gets beneath the level of hiding.

Because of these ground rules mutual support is provided, and an individual's sense of personhood is enhanced, When he is known and appreciated for his real self—when not only his name but some of his innermost feelings and attitudes and problems are known—and yet he is loved and accepted, he begins to sense the preciousness of his unique humanity.

Some Personal Responses to Christian Actualization

One person in a Christian actualization group, while vacationing at the Grand Canyon, wrote his response to what had taken place.

[4] Gerald Anderson, "The Group Member Becomes a Servant," *Pastoral Psychology*, June, 1964, p. 20.

My evaluation of the Christian actualization group is very much like the Grand Canyon this morning—at times completely obscured by clouds of doubt, but at other times patches of understanding and tremendous vistas of future potential are seen, but it's hard to keep them in view because of the cloud of unanswered questions—most of which are really unanswerable because they fit into the category of "what if."

This is a fair evaluation. At this stage in our journey there are still a lot of questions. We have not come upon a program that we would propose for every church. The church is too dynamic and changing. We have experimented with and are seeking to establish a style that is valid both for the individual and for the congregation. We think it would be helpful now to share some experiences of those who have participated in Christian actualization groups. The approach is not theoretical —it has been used to open the life vistas of people like yourself. What they say, they are saying to you.

Although these statements are written in retrospect and do not reveal the everyday struggle of growth and awareness, they are expressions of a recognition of new life—sometimes dramatic.

THE EXPERIENCE OF AN ALTERED SELF-IMAGE

"One of the primary reasons for the improvement in my relationships and communication is my new understanding of the importance of feeling and emotion gained in the Christian actualization group. Prior to this experinece I believed that control of feelings was necessary, particularly for a man, since a man should not let emotion play any significant part in his actions or relationships. I believed that logic was the only thing a man could base his decision on.

161

"Through the group I was able to realize the tremendous importance of the feelings and emotions that I was persistently denying. As I came to the awareness that trying to ignore these strong forces in my life was damaging me and others, I began to change.

"I have been helped to express not only my safe feelings, but also the feelings which I have desperately attempted to keep hidden.

"One benefit of the Christian actualization experience is a renewed and deepening relationship with my wife. We can now deal with the real issues that concern us and not just hide on the surface. Now I am much less prone to restrain my hostile or angry feelings until I reach the breaking point.

"In addition to learning about the centrality of feelings and emotion and sensitivity in relationships, I have discovered something extremely valuable about my faith and Christianity. I now know that to be a Christian is not simply to establish a spiritual or otherworldly relationship with God, but to establish deep human relationships with his children of whom I am one. These relationships must be rooted in love and concern as were the relationships of Christ.

"Because of my growth in sensitivity to the needs and feelings of others, I am now able to enter into their lives and to allow them to enter into mine in a much more helpful way."

AN EXPERIENCE OF NEW VALUES AND INSIGHTS

"I am a manipulator. It is difficult for me to accept this fact, for I believed that my life was completely satisfactory. How wrong I was! How foolish! How unrealistic! As a result of this Christian actualization experience, life—the reality of it—exploded in my face!

"I came into the experience with the subtle feeling that something was wrong with my life. My life was not fulfilling, but I did not know where to begin to search for a more fulfilling way. My marriage, which I had previously thought *perfect*, was now on the rocks. I felt the rejection of my wife, but I did not understand the problem.

"I turned to the church for help and was invited to participate in a Christian actualization group. Fortunately the minister who participated in the group did not quote meaningless garbage that only appeals to the intellect but instead responded as a full human being. As a result, a deeply understanding relationship was developed. I was encouraged to respond on a gut-level basis. Biblical frills and moralizing were spared me, and we got down to the nitty-gritty of my feelings.

"Being honest with another and, more important, with myself was almost beyond my mental endurance. How easy it would have been to run! How badly I wanted to! But I stayed. This was the experience I most needed.

"With the help of the group I became aware that I had been fooling myself for years about the kind of person I was. I lived in the past and the future. I needed to discover how to live fully in the present. Being goal oriented, I had never allowed myself the joy of struggling to discover myself.

"I began to see that with my wife I had the pattern of playing under-dog, weakling, and clinging vine. To compensate for my inadequacies, I resorted to playing judge and also attempted to control my wife through increased sexual demands. Often I have manipulated so as not to have to take risks with my feelings.

"Now I am learning to relate in more positive, actualizing, and Christian ways. During a period of despair over the result of my manipulations, Christ became real to me. A way out of my unfulfilling relationships to myself, others, and God began to emerge.

"As my awareness of myself has increased, I have become more aware of others. It is as though I had reversed the momentum of a giant space ball that previously bounced and bumped against the directional flow of the universe. That space ball was me. Now I am moving away from protectiveness, insensitivity, coldness, frustration, and insecurity and toward awareness, warmth, sensitivity, and happiness. Now people are no longer things or objects but warm, alive, and important persons.

"I feel that I am different now; it is not only my feelings that have changed but the entirety of my selfhood. I now believe that within me is a 'spark of the divine,' and the Christian actualization group has helped me to fan and ignite that spark."

A YOUTH BRIDGES THE GENERATION GAP [5]

"After a few weeks in the experimental group, I discovered that these adults were not relating as incoherent schoolteachers or parents but that they were relating to each other and to me as authentic, trusting, human beings. As we became more sensitive to the human aspects that are similar in each of us, we became much more able to risk our real selves with the rest of the group.

"We became able not only to share our problems and our negativity but also our joyful affirmation and the 'good news.' For the first time in my life I am experiencing an inner trust

[5] This response came from a youth in an experimental worship fellowship of an actualizing nature.

164

which I discovered only through the process of risk and confrontation.

"In this experience I was able to realize and admit to myself and to the others many of my manipulations. This self-revelation in the company of adults as well as my peers has opened me to the possibility of becoming more actualizing. The thing that surprised me about this group was that I too was expected to share in the leadership of confession and adoration and was valued for my contribution."

Epilogue
A Continuous Rebirth

To conclude our journey, we would like to refer to Alan Watts's contrast between belief and faith. Belief is the insistence in the here and now, that this is what one values and subscribes to in terms of his present limited experience. *Belief* must be amplified by *faith*. Faith does not simply defend the truth as one sees it now, but faith is, in Watts's words, "an unreserved opening of the mind to the truth, whatever it may turn out to be. Faith has not preconceptions; it is a plunge into the unknown. Belief clings but faith lets go."

The journey of actualization requires death as well as rebirth—death to outworn ideas and beliefs, death to outdated structures, death to irrelevant modes of worship and service; above all, death to manipulative relationships. The process is not simply a once-and-for-all rebirth, but rather a continuing rebirth, where the old self is continually dying and the new self is continually being born and continually being discovered and expressed.

The process of this continuous rebirth is akin to the process of continuous birth and death of cells in the body, which is required if the body is to grow. Life is like a melody which is produced by both the sounding and the silencing of individual notes. The greater life, therefore, is not made up simply of living—but a process of both living and dying.

The nature of "being-born" is described unusually well by Erich Fromm:

Birth is not one act; it is a process. The aim of life is to be fully born, though its tragedy is that most of us die before we are thus born. To live is to be born every minute. Death occurs when birth stops. . . . The other answer is to be *fully born*, to develop one's awareness, one's reason, one's capacity to love, to such a point that one transcends one's own egocentric involvement, and arrives at a new harmony, at a new oneness with the world."[1]

Samuel Miller talks about it in this fashion:

For a man's birth is not ended with the first gasp of his breath and the first cry of his lungs. He is born for innumerable births. He is forever pushing his way into new worlds. Through countless experiences, by high ecstasies and deep sorrows he plunges to new heights and depths within himself. Through the old symbols and the new insights he sees fresh and alluring vistas. Grief and love lead him far beyond himself. Prophets and poets shout across the ages and call out his soul. Beauty unseals his eyes and reverence leads him to mystery and tenderness. The strange designs of circumstances and purpose, the impact of this world and all its wonders, the dark movings of the inner abyss in himself, all these are avenues of births beyond number.[2]

[1] D. T. Suzuki, Erich Fromm, and Richard De Martino, *Zen Buddhism & Psychoanalysis* (New York: Harper & Brothers, 1960), pp. 88, 87.
[2] *Life of the Soul* (New York: Harper & Row, 1951), pp. 136-37.

As we have the courage to communicate with others with whom we differ, the courage to open ourselves in honesty and awareness, we develop also the courage to kill off old preconceptions. Faith requires an opening of ourselves to new ideas and new involvements, a willingness to let old outworn ideas and habits die. This is what Tillich means by the "courage to doubt." One must develop the courage to entertain differences in the hope that one may learn new and satisfying ways of viewing truth. The actualizing person is unlike the manipulator, who builds a narrow castle of certitude which is defended with the utmost tenacity. He expresses and asks so that he can receive in his areas of doubt—risking that the answers will probably not come easily, but that he will have to work out his own salvation each day with fear and trembling. This being so, each day is an encounter of reality in his ongoing dying-and-being-born adventure in living.

The great hope is that from the actualization group within the church may come the true *koinonia*. While the actualization group serves deep fundamental needs and can be one of the saving forces for the modern church, we will have stopped short of fulfillment if from the actualization efforts real *koinonia* does not come.

From this experience of *koinonia*, actualizing Christians move out into *diakonia*. This mission is characterized by honest relationships, personal involvement, and authentic caring. The arena is changed from the actualization group to the relationships of day-to-day existence. Such relationships are not programmed and deliberate, for the road from manipulative Christianity to actualizing Christianity is one from deadness to aliveness, and from deliberateness to spontaneity.

For Further Help

Information on the workshops, materials, and films listed below is available from the Institute of Therapeutic Psychology and from Psychological Films, Inc., both at 205 W. 20th Street, Santa Ana, California 92706.

Workshops

Training workshop. A special three-week training course for ministers and psychologists interested in conducting actualization groups is provided during the summer and by special arrangements during the year. This course is conducted by the writers and Dr. Robert Hilton, coordinator of training for the Institute of Therapeutic Psychology.

Experiential Worship Workbook. A collection of services based on the Beatitudes in relation to the actualization process. Contains also other services and experiments in relationships to enhance worship and assist the church in becoming actualization-centered.

Self-Actualization Workbook, by Everett L. Shostrom and the staff of Institute of Therapeutic Psychology. A specially designed workbook for conducting a self-actualization workshop. Twelve two-hour sessions are designed. Included are materials for each session.

Films

1. "The Actualization Group." This is a startling new film series showing an authentic, unrehearsed therapy or sensitivity group. This series was originally presented on KHJ-TV in Los Angeles by Everett L. Shostrom, Ph.D., and Nancy W. Ferry, M.S.W. This series was planned so that the viewer follows one group through seven sessions of therapy. Thus the viewer is able to study the group process through the series.

2. "Maslow and Self-actualization." Abraham Maslow, founder of the concept of self-actualization, discusses the various dimensions of self-actualization which he has heretofore written about. It is illustrated by the life of an individual deemed to be self-actualizing.

3. "Three Approaches to Psychotherapy." A three-part film series illustrating three distinguished approaches to psychotherapy. Film No. 1 is devoted to Dr. Carl Rogers; Film No. 2, Dr. Frederick Perls; and Film No. 3, Dr. Albert Ellis. Each therapist describes his system of therapy. He then demonstrates his work with a patient—Gloria—and finally comments briefly on his interview.

4. "Search and Search: Psychology in Perspective." An introduction to psychotherapy and its historical background. Through the medium of a young lady who seeks psychotherapy, the film describes the three forces of psychology: experimental, psychoanalytic, and existential or humanistic psychology. Illustrated by film clips of Carl Rogers, Rollo May, and Harry Harlow.

5. "Target Five." A film of the work of Virginia Satir, the nationally acclaimed family therapist, integrated with the work of Dr. Shostrom, the founder of actualization therapy. In dialogue, they integrate each of their concepts.

6. "Rollo May and Human Encounter." In this film "Mr. Humanist," Dr. Rollo May, presents his two-part concept of

human encounter; the self-self encounter and the self-other encounter.

7. "Frederick Perls and Human Awareness." In this two-part film series Dr. Perls first presents the key concepts of Gestalt therapy, which relates to human awareness. In the second part he demonstrates his concepts with a group and for individuals.

Books of Special Value

Brammer, Lawrence M., and Shostrom, Everett L. *Therapeutic Psychology—Principles of Actualization Counseling and Psychotherapy.* 2nd. ed. Englewood Cliffs, N.J.: Prentice-Hall, 1968.

Frankl, Viktor E. *Man's Search for Meaning.* New York: Washington Square Press, 1963.

Hoekendijk, J. C. *The Church Inside Out.* Philadelphia: The Westminster Press, 1966.

Hulme, William E. *Your Pastor's Problems: A Guide for Ministers and Laymen.* Garden City, N.Y.: Doubleday & Co., 1966.

Leslie, Robert C. *Jesus and Logotherapy.* Nashville: Abingdon Press, 1965.

Maguire, John David. *The Dance of the Pilgrim.* New York: Association Press, 1967.

Maslow, Abraham H. *Toward a Psychology of Being.* Princeton: D. Van Nostrand Co., 1962.

Shostrom, Everett L. *Man, the Manipulator.* Nashville: Abingdon Press, 1967.

Snyder, Ross. *On Becoming Human.* Nashville: Abingdon Press, 1967.

Index

173

DATE DUE

DATE DUE			
MAR 31 '70			
APR 22 '70			
JUN 4 '70			
OCT 21 '74			
NOV 9 '85			
FEB 5 '88			
FEB 26 '88			
MAR 7 '88			

DEMCO 38-297